SELF-SUFFICIENT COUNTRY LIVING

By the Same Author

THE PERSONAL PRINCIPLE
THE WITHERED BRANCH

D.S. SAVAGE

SELF-SUFFICIENT COUNTRY LIVING

St. Martin's Press/New York

For Mark, Chris, and Ted

Design by Lynn Braswell
Library of Congress Cataloging in Publication Data

Savage, Derek S
☐ Self-suffcient country living.
1. Country Life——Great Britain——Handbooks, manuals, ets.
2. Country Life——Handbooks, manuals, etc.
S513.2.S28 1975b   630'.941
76-28057
ISBN 0-312-71249-9 (Paper)
ISBN 0-312-71248-0 (Cloth)

Contents

v

Introduction

When William Cobbett wrote his eminently practical *Cottage Economy* nearly a century and a half ago it was to instruct the farm laborer of that time in ways and means of regaining some of his diminished well-being and independence. The present book has to a large extent drawn its inspiration from Cobbett's manual of self-help. The immense changes of the past 150 years have eliminated the old-style farmer and farm laborer. The countryside has become depopulated while the towns have become crammed with the descendants of the disinherited countryman. There is now coming into being a new type of cottager, the townsman in revolt against an industrial-commercial society, seeking a way of life simple and self-reliant. It is for this "cottager" that this book has been written.

It has long seemed to me that the real trouble with our present society is that it has lost its human centrality, that impersonal processes are allowed to expand without reference to the real needs of human beings, and no one seems able to stop this happening. The paradox is that nobody really desires the social effects of these processes, although they take them as inevitable, the price to be paid for progress. Progress towards what? So-called progress is running into difficulties, perhaps disaster on a world scale.

A good deal has been written in recent years on the wastefulness of a consumer society making inroads into limited natural resources, and pollution of the environment as these resources are turned into consumer goods. Less attention has been given to the mindless destruction of its own earlier stages by a highly progressive economy. Yet common sense and a calm self-interest should have seen to it that much of the technology of the eighteenth and nineteenth centuries—the development of hydraulics and steam power—was carried forward into the present. This shortsightedness now threatens the further devaluation of man. There may perhaps be ways in which pressure can be brought to bear to check these ominous trends, but such organized effort takes time to make itself felt, and in the meantime the need for men and women to live in as positive and humanly creative a way as they can remains undiminished. A sense of personal accountability for his actions may lead an individual here and there to live in stubborn disregard of the pressure to antlike conformity, and from such partial detachment from the way of life of the urban collective it is only one more step to move out of the town into the countryside. On grounds of practicality and common sense this has much to recommend it. If collective civilization is heading for a slow, grinding halt it helps neither civilization nor oneself to go under with it.

Cobbett, who took it for granted that country life was superior to the life of towns, and who never spoke of London but as "the great wen," even in 1821, did not have to argue the point with his readers: they were, of course, countrymen. Nor shall I attempt to do so. If a man is wedded to the town it is useless to try to make a countryman of him. I shall assume that my reader is an actual or intending cottager. I intend to give him, if he thinks he needs it, some useful instruction in the humble and down-to-earth practicalities of day-to-day country living. Compared with Cobbett, however, I am at a double disadvantage in that I can take for granted neither my readers' uniformity of circumstance or needs, nor their basic acquaintance with country ways.

In a time of rapid social change I have felt obliged to write with one eye on present conditions of relative stability and the other on a possible future state of relative scarcity. There will therefore be some unavoidable contradictions and inconsistencies in what I write, since I hope my book may be of use both in the present and the near future. Who knows what tomorrow may bring? Certainly not I, nor, I suspect, the reader. This ignorance applies even to the rather basic matter of the availability of the country cottage. Twenty years ago it was still possible in most parts of the country to rent an empty farm cottage without modern conveniences for a few dollars a week. Today, at least in coastal and mountain areas, such places have fallen into the hands mainly of car-owning weekenders from the cities who have modernized them out of recognition and used them as second homes. It is anyone's guess what the position will be in 10 or 20 years' time: all we can be sure of is that it will be very different from what it is now. I have taken my aim to be not to instruct the reader how and where to look for a cottage but how to cope with the facts of life when he has got one.

In any cottage way of life the garden is the most important thing. The larger the garden the greater the degree of self-support which will be possible. A cottage which has, in addition to a garden, a meadow or orchard, or grazing rights on common land, offers much greater opportunities. An intending cottager should always try for as large a parcel of land as possible when negotiating for a dwelling. Not all cottagers are so fortunate as to live in houses attached to shoreline, lakeside, mountain slopes or forest land, but some do. Even surrounded by arable fields the cottager will have some access to lanes, marshes or woodlands with attendant advantages. But however sizable his holding, he would be unwise to depend upon the sale of its products to provide a cash income. He should rather aim at supplying most of his own needs with a surplus for barter or sale. If he has a spare half or quarter acre on which to grow a specially profitable crop for a cash return—one which might pay rent,—taxes, mortgage interest or grocer's bill, perhaps from the sale of flowers, mushrooms, strawberries, rhubarb or horseradish—he should keep in mind that any year the crop may fail or the market collapse. An independent source of income which links him to the general economy, even if it be a small income, is essential. Cobbett's farm laborer after all had his weekly wage. In today's conditions one is well advised to have a foot in both camps. If worse comes to worse, the foot firmly planted in the rural world will enable a cottager to feed his family and himself while giving him a base for recovery.

I am not, then, writing for the would-be small farmer, the market gardener,* or even the man Americans call the "homesteader." I am writing for the ordinary cottager who may have no more than the average-sized garden but who has the incomparable advantage of living in the countryside rather than the environment of the town. There are

* See glossary for unfamiliar terms

many computations of productivity in keeping livestock, cultivating land and the employment of the
hours of daylight, but few of these will be found to
have a useful bearing since individual circumstances
such as climate, the nature of the soil and the crops
that can be grown are variables. Some notion of the
possibilities of large-scale cottaging enterprise may
be arrived at if we assume a 1-acre garden
supplemented by livestock. In terms of additional
land the cottager would need roughly:

for 2 goats:	1120 lb hay requiring ¼ acre land
	560 lb grain requiring ¼ acre land
for 2 pigs kept 6 months:	1568 lb grain re-
	quiring ⅔ acre land
for 12 hens:	896 lb grain requiring ⅜ acre land
for rabbits:	say 560 lb hay requiring ⅛ acre land
	280 lb grain requiring ⅛ acre land

The total, including garden, comes to 3 acres. If
we then add another acre for pasture for goats and
½-acre pasture for hens and pigs, all of which can
be kept in a more confined area if need be, we find
that a holding of about 4½ acres is plenty large
enough to produce all the food, except such
groceries as sugar, tea, coffee, pepper, salt and
spices, as may be needed by a medium-sized family
living at a high meat-eating standard and working
the land intensively and efficiently. A smaller family eating little or no meat but requiring eggs, milk,
butter and cheese would need less land, and still

less if they had the means to buy in hay and grain. A semivegetarian one would need even less. In any case the vegetable garden must be central to the economy. Here the heaviest labor is digging, the second heaviest harvesting, particularly in handling bulky crops like potatoes and apples. There are various ways of lightening the load and in any event digging is mostly done from autumn to early spring when there is little other work. Mechanical cultivators should in my opinion be left to market gardeners, not only because of capital cost and mounting running expenses but because their use can be justified for only a very short period in the year. The rare cottager with a holding large enough to fall into the market gardening or smallholder class would be well advised to consider animal power— the horse, the pony, even the donkey. In farming there are some indications that the working horse may be making a slow comeback in certain places. The homesteader cottager will find that the working pony costs little to keep. It will live on hay and grass and sleep out of doors all the year round if required although it will be a better worker if stabled and given crushed oats and bran. Donkeys are useful beasts of burden and can be used as draft animals and for light plowing and harrowing, as they are in some "backward" countries today. Alas, like the goat, they have been looked upon by the pampered and snobbish as low-caste and therefore ridiculous. Donkeys are, however, very economical and intelligent beasts. They live as long as 30 years and the females can be bred from up to the age of 20, the gestation period being 11 months. They will need ½ acre of pasture each with hay and greenstuff in winter supplemented with a handful of concentrate a day. They require no shoeing but must be groomed. And what about the ox? Perhaps the day of the ox may yet return, for a team of oxen plows as well as a team of horses and will thrive on a diet of straw, roots and a small amount of meal— the starvation line for a working horse!

Without animals, far more can be done by hard labor than most people suppose; nor is the labor tiring or unpleasant once one's muscles are used to it and one can go at it at one's own pace. If he has some seasonal help with beet hoeing, fruit picking and harvesting, one healthy man can manage a much bigger area of land than the uninitiated would think possible. He can also enjoy a varied diet, a healthy open-air life with no lack of occupation and yet leisure for reading, writing, music and conversation. No well-paid city job could ever give him such a sense of well-being, and in fact the chief danger of this combination of agriculture and horticulture is that it can become too absorbing.

Apart from husbandry there are other matters of concern to the cottager. Some of the subjects I have dealt with in this book may not be liked by some people, and I may be asked why I have included a chapter on growing tobacco in view of the hazard of lung cancer, on brewing when the dangers of alcoholism are widely recognized. My answer is that if people will smoke and drink it is better for them to smoke their own tobacco and drink their own beer than that packaged for them by manufacturers. No one need do so if he doesn't want to. It will be apparent that when I describe how to keep and kill a pig, hen or rabbit, I am not writing for strict vegetarians or people who regard all killing of animals as criminal. While I would personally counsel moderation in the eating of flesh foods and would agree with those who point out that it is more economical to feed grain direct to human beings than to human beings through the bodies of animals, I do not regard the domestication and killing of animals as iniquitous. It would not be easy to maintain such an attitude in the conditions of rural life where pests of all sorts have to be destroyed to protect crops and stock, and unwanted male animals slaughtered to maintain a balance and maximum productivity. Many people who would scorn the meat of squirrel or sparrow but would dine on quail, woodcock or rabbit make this distinction as a result of unconscious social or cultural prejudice. Should our level of culture again regress as it did in the last war we might find ourselves eating not Swiss chard from the Victory garden but sparrows, starlings and squirrels, as is still the case among the rural poor. By general admission, the world food crisis is here to stay, even in wealthy America, where soaring prices and unpredictable shortages of staples have become facts of life for most people.

Not only the vegetarian but the sportsman may be offended by some of the material in these pages unless he grasps that I have deliberately taken no account of his point of view. My concern is with the elementary practicalities of life in the country. Sport being essentially an activity in which the means employed take precedence over the end pursued, I cannot do otherwise than take a practical view. My instructions for the easy taking of beasts, birds and fishes are given with a view to possible times of scarcity. The cottager, like everyone else, is bound to obey the laws of the society in which he lives; he is bound also to act in accordance with his conscience. In telling the reader how a thing may be done I am not necessarily, even by implication, telling him to go out and do it. I am not saying that under all circumstances, or in particular circumstances, he may do so. This is something he must decide for himself.

No book such as this can tell the intending countryman *all* he needs to know. Limitations of space have compelled me to leave out some subjects which might otherwise have been included, but I have tried to write clearly and concisely about matters which I know from experience are of concern to the beginning cottager.

D.S.S.

Part I:

FRIENDS, FOES AND ESSENTIAL AMENITIES

□ 1 □

VERMIN

The town dweller pays his taxes and in return expects a number of services from municipal employees, including the collection of garbage, the disposal of sewage and the suppression of pests and vermin. In the countryside it is different. The rural dweller with an acre or two of land will have to defend himself against four-footed enemies and winged raiders with an alertness the need for which increases the further he gets from his fellow man. At the edge of a suburb or within a village there may be few enemies. In open country there are predators who take for granted their right to share the contents of his garden and the stores of house and barn. The fox and the rat, as well as the hawk and the crow, may prey on his poultry, chicks and eggs. The rabbit may burrow under his fence and ravage the greenstuff and roots in his garden. Mice and rats will get at his grain and feed stores.

Blackbirds will eat whatever they fancy from his garden. Sparrows and finches will dig up seeds and peck out the centers from fruit buds, while jays will rip beans and peas from their pods.

First let us separate friends from enemies; and then, among the enemies, those to be outwitted or warned off, from those to be destroyed.

Garden friends to be encouraged are the frog and the toad. Among insects: the ladybird, the hoverfly, the ichneumon fly, the lacewing, the centipede (not millipede), the ground beetle and the rove beetle.

Garden foes to be discouraged are: birds of nearly every kind, and besides the harmful creatures already named, moles, meadow mice, badgers, foxes, squirrels, and of course, cats and dogs, straying cows, goats and horses. Animals are best kept off by tight gates and fences, and birds by netting where appropriate and by various forms of bird scarers, like threads of cotton stretched tightly along the tops of growing seedlings, rattling tins, and foil which flashes and crackles in the breeze. They can also be discouraged by dosing seeds with nasty-tasting chemicals, paints or oil before sowing, and by doing away with conditions which favor the presence of the pest in question.

Insects apart, garden and house enemies to be destroyed where all else fails are: rats, mice, rabbits, foxes, and whatever non protected birds pose a threat to food supplies. These include: crows, magpies, and starlings, house sparrows and jays.

Unless the latter three are doing great damage, they, along with songbirds, may generally not be killed. Animal predators include: foxes, coyotes, bobcats, mountain lions, domestic cats, rats, weasals and opossums. The badger and the mole are classed as predators, yet are all but harmless.

● **Fences.** The first thing that a new owner or tenant in the country must do is to go round the boundaries of his property and look at the fences. The best barriers against intruders are brick and stone walls. Oak fencing, open or close, is good, the protection it gives depending on its height and thickness. The most pleasing boundary is a live hedge. Hawthorn and holly are the most stockproof, but beech, hazel, maple and hornbeam all make stout hedges of quick growth. Plant a row of healthy seedlings 8 in. apart, manure them freely the first year, then cut them right back the following year. Trim the sides of the new hedge as it grows, leaving the top shoots to grow to the required height before heading. A wire fence may be needed while they are growing. Don't use barbed wire. A plain fence of wire strands tightly strained will keep out sheep and cattle. The end or corner posts must be staunch; make them rigid with diagonal spurs or struts to take the strain and see that they are well pickled with creosote or tar. They may then be embedded in concrete or in a socket made by four large stones. Wood fence posts should always have their bases charred in the fire and coated with tar or pitch to prevent rot. A cheap fence is split chestnut paling, sold in rolls and erected by wiring it at intervals to iron stakes sledged into the ground. There are several kinds of chain link and welded mesh fences, some with small mesh at the bottom to keep out rodents and wide mesh at the top. Generally the price of such fences is in inverse proportion to the size of their mesh: i.e., the smaller the mesh the more they cost per yard.

Where rabbits abound, firm measures are needed to keep them outside. Unless defended by brick or stone, your garden needs to be enclosed by wire netting of 1-in. mesh, at least 3 feet above ground level, with 6 in. or more buried to prevent the beasts from tunneling under it. Guard against baby rabbits as well as adults. A good wooden fence need have the netting only at its foot—use 2-ft. high netting, 1 ft. being let into the ground and the rest stapled to the wood on the outside of the fence. The same can be done with fences of other types. With living hedges the netting is fixed independently on the inner or garden side, the top edge being bent over outwards and so fixed with brackets to hinder rabbits from climbing it. Rabbits hate onions, so a border of any of the onion family all round the garden will help to keep them off it. Like birds, rats, moles and meadow mice cannot be kept out by any sort of hedge or wall. No fence is stronger than its weakest point. When making a wire netting fence, as in chicken runs, get some plain 8-gauge wire and interweave one strand at the top and one near the bottom throughout its length. These may be stretched taut without damage to the netting, which itself cannot be stretched or tightened. A third wire will strengthen the netting against stock. A gate in the fence must be kept shut always, and a solid concrete or timber sill laid on the ground exactly parallel with its bottom and so fitted that there is no room for a rabbit to squeeze through. Weasels will attack young chickens if they can get at them through ordinary 2-in. wire netting. Chickens killed at night may be the victims of a rat which has taken up residence inside the hen house; it must be found and killed without delay.

● **Firearms.** A gun may be the only way of keeping down rabbits, rats, crows and weasels which have become serious pests. Guns used are the air rifle, the .22 rifle and the double-barrel 12-bore shotgun with 26-in. or 30-in. barrels. Check with your local Game Department about licenses for these. The air gun is not always effective, and the bullet from the .22 rifle is too dangerous inside a mile range. This leaves the shotgun, and if used only for shooting in the garden and yard then the smaller make of .410 caliber, the "four-ten" is adequate. Some specially light "garden guns" fire cartridges the tubes of which are made of a special paper which separates from the metal head on firing and travels through the bore of the gun intact to disintegrate from the muzzle, leaving the shot to travel on. These are especially suited for use in confined spaces where a more powerful gun would cause structural damage. Killing pests is not a form of sport, so sitting targets should be chosen; to shoot on the wing may mean wounding a bird which must then die a lingering death outside the garden.

Rabbits in the garden are elusive, dodging about under cover in the vegetable patch. Try for a sitting shot in early morning and just before dusk.

Rats are easier to hit. They will climb up bean and pea rows at any time of day but are best hunted in the evening. In winter they move into buildings, migrating in summer to burrows in hedge banks. Their burrows have smaller entrance holes than rabbits', and their dung, usually found near these holes, resembles rabbits' but is elongated and dark in color. They can be attacked in their holes by ferrets, who drive them out for dogs to kill.

● **Snaring rabbits and rats.** The use of snares is described on page 226. It is not so easy to see the rabbit's tracks in garden soil as on turf, but if the rabbit is "guided" along a low wire netting fence with a wire set in each opening, he will be caught. Snares may be set for rats, but where rabbits require a three-strand wire and a 4-in. noose, the rat snare need be of only two strands or one, with a 2-in. noose. Refer to the passage on snaring rabbits, set up the same sort of snare for rats but add to it a "bender" in the form of a stout hazel rod about 4 ft. long, to the top of which is tied the string of the snare. Fasten a piece of wood with a transverse notch to the string close to the edge of the wire. Drive a peg with an engaging notch slantwise into the ground. Bend down the hazel switch and engage the notches so that they will come apart at a light pull on the wire. Then set the snare, with a little cleft stick, across a rat run or at the mouth of a hole. The rat runs his head into the noose and pulls apart the notched pieces, the bender flies upwards and jerks the loop tightly round his neck, and the wretch is neatly gallowed. A snare of this pattern, able to lift 18 lbs, will do for foxes. Foxes are wary foes, and if one has to be dealt with it is best to pursue several methods—shooting, snaring and trapping—at once.

● **Rats, mice and moles.** Rats and mice may be caught in patent traps of the spring or cage type. And they may be poisoned. It is generally illegal to poison rabbits and other animals, though a property owner may sometimes obtain permission to do so if the animals are doing substantial harm. Rats may be gassed by connecting a hosepipe with the exhaust of a car or mower and running its other end to one of the holes in a burrow, the other holes being first stopped with earth. Start the engine and let it run for a while and the rats will be killed by the lethal gases which will filter through the whole run system—clear proof of the noxiousness of the fumes which we put up with in our city streets. Moles can be driven away from their runs by this means if their exit holes are left unstopped. Smoke cartridges against moles may be bought in hardware and farm supply stores. A large onion cut in half and wedged in a mole run is said to send them away, since moles cannot abide strong stinks. (As they are blind, it cannot make them weep.) The village mole catcher, who trapped moles and made up their downy skins into men's vests, is now a figure of the past, but mole traps may be bought in most rural hardware stores.

Once rats have got into a building they are difficult to dislodge. Make sure that all walls of a house are rat proof, and look at all air bricks and metal gratings which ventilate its foundations, as well as openings under eave boards, and put them to rights. Rats will get into thatched roofs; hence the wire netting sometimes used to cover such roofs to keep them out. Wooden sheds and outhouses must be protected at ground level by brick or concrete footings. If these are lacking, the remedy is to fix small-mesh wire netting all round the walls, sunk 1 ft. into the ground and rising 1 ft. above it, stapling the upper part to the side of the shed. Rats may be prevented from gnawing a gap at the bottom of a door by a strip of sheet metal screwed along the outer side, coming down to within ½ in. of the sill. The danger from rats in case of social breakdown and plague should be considered, and steps taken now to make all one's buildings rat proof.

Where rats are attracted to kitchen waste in compost boxes they can be poisoned by a sprinkling of gypsum on the rubbish or deterred by chloride of lime. Mice can be kept from food by the crushed leaves of goutweed.

Inside or outside, rats and mice are best dealt with by a not too well fed cat, preferably female, of the old-fashioned hunting strain. A fox terrier will deal effectively with the biggest rat. These creatures are more efficient than traps, baits and poisons; and every countryman knows that no home is complete without a cat and a dog.

● **Insect pests.** Cockroaches can be got rid of by strewing on the floor before bedtime a mixture of crushed gypsum with twice the quantity of sugared oatmeal. Beetles can be poisoned with a mixture of equal weights of red lead, sugar and flour. Green flies: keep them away from the ice chest by placing a saucer of water and permanganate of potash near its door. Mosquitoes: drive them from the room by holding a lump of camphor gum over a lamp chimney. Flies: attract and destroy them by strong, sweet green tea set about the room in saucers. Ants are repelled by the herbs pennyroyal, spearmint and tansy. Destroy ants by dropping quicklime on their nest entrance and washing it in with boiling water. Carpet and clothes moths are repelled by the scent of dried lavender. Clothes in a closet may be sprinkled with dried leaves of lavender, mint, rosemary, sage and wormwood to keep moths away.

□ 2 □

STONE WALL AND
HAWTHORN HEDGE

It sometimes happens that part of a country property has a stone wall in need of extension or repair,
or a thorn hedge that has been let go and must be
laid, or layered, to make it animal proof.

● **Stone walls** (Fig. 1) are found in places where a
rocky substrate lies close to the soil surface, with
outcrops and loose stones here and there. Walls
around fields have usually been built originally with
stones lifted from the field itself, supplemented by
stones from a nearby quarry. When building a drystone wall—"dry" because no mortar is used—the
first thing is to sort out the stones into sizes and to
arrange that supplies shall be carried or drawn by
sled downhill rather than up. Treat walling as a
summer rather than a winter job.

Peg a double line where the wall is to run and

23

dig a 6–8-in.-deep foundation trench, paving it with stones a bit wider than the base of the wall at ground level. Tools needed besides spade and line will be an expanding rule, a 4-lb. club hammer, a cold chisel, a mallet and an iron crowbar—with a thick 6-ft.-long plank and a length of rope if heavy stones are to be hauled and levered into place.

Walls are built with two parallel rows of stones fitted closely together, and the rule is to lay each stone on its broadest face lengthwise into the wall, placing the larger stones in the lower courses, the size of the stones getting smaller towards the top of the wall, the wall being "battered" (sloped), each side at an angle of 10°. It follows that a wall with a 34-in. base will be 20 in. wide at 3 ft. 9 in. high, or 14 in. wide at 6 ft. Such a wall can be built up at any time without having to be pulled down and rebuilt. If the wall is a long one, fix into the ground at each end timber frames the exact shape of the wall to be built, with guide strings stretched from one to the other, and work within the strings.

Not more than two foundation stones make the width of the trench. Follow them with further layers, each sloped inwards a little and so placed as to cover the joint in the lower course. Work from each side in turn and fill in any space between the two sides with small rubble packed tight. The art is to select stones that will fit into each other, with a smooth face on the flank of the wall. At about 21 in. from the ground, large rectangular "tie stones" as long as the wall's width must be placed across it at 3-ft. intervals to hold the two sides together. The course is made up with smaller irregular stones and the building continued as before. If the wall is to be 6 ft. high, then further tie stones will be put in at about 4 ft. Whole stones are best, but if a tie stone has to be cut, score a groove along all four faces

Fig. 1

with a cold chisel and hammer; then, placing a board upright over the groove, strike it a few blows on its edge with the mallet. Stone fresh from the quarry is the easiest to work. A 4-ft. wall can be finished by covering it at about 3 ft. 3 in. high with flat single stones and then capping it with flat vertical stones of roughly equal size stacked tightly edgewise. Put in a heavy stone here and there to hold them in case some are knocked out. Go along the finished wall and hammer small stones into all gaps. If skillfully built, such a wall will stand for decades without attention. Where stone abounds, the art of walling can be applied to the erection of large or small buildings, stones being raised to the upper levels by block and tackle or the use of the power lift on a tractor.

Where stone is scarce, concrete blocks tongued and grooved for rigid fitting together may be made in a wooden mold and used instead. As an alternative, gunny sack halves may be stitched into narrow bags and filled with a sand/cement mixture, then stacked up dry to make the wall. A heavy rainstorm will set them hard, or they can be hosed or doused with water as the wall is built.

● **Laying a hedge** (Fig. 2). A field hedge often has a drainage ditch on the outer boundary; and the winter work of laying a thorn hedge so that it grows in such a way as to be proof against stock is done where possible from the ditch side. The hedger wears tough leather gloves, uses a billhook to sever the wood and a mallet to knock in any non-live stakes that may be wanted. The work is essentially that of selecting, bending and weaving the layers semihorizontally and in one direction between the vertical dead or living stakes, the job being finished off by binding or braiding the top of the hedge with headers—long lengths of live or dead stem 1/2–3/4 in. thick.

Without doubt the best hedge is an all-living one in which stakes, layers and headers are all selected

Fig. 2

and trimmed from the live wood. But it is quite usual to have only the layers live, cutting the stakes and headers from waste hedge material or buying them from the owner of a coppice in bundles holding enough to do a chain at a time.

Proceed like this: (1) First clear the hedge bottom of brambles and other rubbish, cut out unwanted growth at the sides and chop out all old, useless stumps from the hedgerow. (2) Thin the hedge, not too severely at first, leaving untouched all stems required for stakes, layers and headers. (3) For stakes, select the thickest stems at about 3-ft. intervals and top them at hedge height. (4) Then work along the hedge, with an upward blow of the billhook cutting each layer as close to the ground as possible and bending it away from the cut, which should be clean and long *but only deep enough to bring the layer down;* otherwise sap flow may be impeded and the layer die. The aim should be to get the hedge to lean slightly over away from the ditch, with the "brush" or small wood pushed through to the field side where it will protect from grazing cattle the young shoots that will later break from the bottom of the hedge. Lay the thorns with an upward slant, bending the lateral growth on them over the other way and weaving it into the fabric of the hedge. (5) If live headers are to be used, leave some very long thin stems every 10 or 12 ft. on the ditch side. When a section of laying is done, cut them upwards at the bottom, like the layers, but bend them in the contrary direction and braid them between the stakes along the hedge top, where they will both strengthen the hedge and hold the layers in place. If dead headers must be used, cut or buy hazel rods 12 ft. by 1½ in. at the butt end, or use strong brambles. Key in the end of each rod so that it cannot work free, and weave it in and out as part of a continuous plait. The best hedge is one which is thick at the bottom, tapering towards the top; and cutting the layers low will aid the growth of shoots from the hedge bottom. Fill a large gap by pegging a layer down to the earth so that it may take root or grow into new stems. At the same time take into account the possibility of keeping here and there any good oak, elm or ash saplings which might grow up into tall hedgerow trees. On finishing the hedge, clean the ditch and throw the soil along the hedge bottom.

Trimming the hedge to keep it in shape is done at odd times throughout the year. Using a slashing hook, trim the hedge with upward sweeps on the sides and with downward strokes at the top.

● **Electric fences** can be a great help when animals are to be contained in a field. They are light and easy to move, and as almost no current is lost from the live wire except when it is grounded by contact with an animal, the same small battery can power an unlimited length of fence. A 6-volt motorcycle battery will last for several months, or the current may be got from the mains. Stranded 24-gauge or 14-gauge plain galvanized wire makes the fence, but any sort of plain wire can be used. Horses and cattle need only one wire to control them; pigs need two, and goats three—but the third, the bottom wire, need not be live.

The tackle needed to fence a ½-acre field for goats is: one fencer unit with battery, one mounting post, four corner tripods, eight ⅜-in. fencer posts, sixteen adjustable insulators, six corner insulators, two wire strainers, one plastic gate handle. For a 1-acre enclosure an extra eight posts and sixteen insulators are needed.

The corner tripods are first set out, the two supporting props standing inwards to take the strain of the wire. The metal mounting post is knocked into the ground, the switched-off fencer unit fixed to it and the battery connected. (The metal post grounds the current: if a wood post is used, a connection to a terminal must be made.) The fence posts are then set out at 12-yd. intervals and the top and middle wires attached to them by the adjustable insulators, the circuit being completed back to the unit. The top wire should be about 30 in. above the ground, at the goats' eye level, the second wire some 18 or 20 in. and the third, the dead wire, 9 in. above ground.

Fig. 3

A gate in the fence (Fig. 3) is made by fixing, about 2 ft. apart, two rigid posts which will take the strain of the fence, by cutting the wire, slipping on the plastic gate handle, then looping the end of the wire so that it can be hooked over to reconnect the circuit at the other side of the gate. (The "gate," that is to say, is just two strands of detachable wire. The gate itself does not take the strain of the fence—if it did, the fence would sag every time it was opened.) The fence wire is now pulled taut by turning the strainers, a tight fence being necessary for making positive skin contact through the animals' hair should they touch the wire. The gate is unhooked, the goats led through, the gate fastened and the current switched on. To train goats to respect the fence, bait the wire with green fodder so that when they first take it they get a shock through the mouth. As the current is not continuous but intermittent, at some forty impulses a minute, it cannot harm them. An electric fence is often used to fold animals on land for controlled grazing of kale, etc., the wire being moved daily to take in a fresh strip of grazing. Rabbits can be very effectively kept out of a field by an electrified fence set 4 in. from the ground.

● **Hurdles.** The cottager who keeps animals of any kind will find it useful to have a dozen sheep hurdles on hand for use when required. They are cheap and take up little space when stacked. A pen for animals—say, for a kidding goat—is quickly made out of four or eight hurdles and four corner posts. Sheep hurdles have a loose iron loop at the top of one end for slipping over a post or stake, and pointed footings which grip the ground; they are surprisingly firm when put together. They make useful temporary gates or fences and can be rigged up into shelters with roofs of corrugated iron or of bracken or straw thatch.

□ 3 □

THE COUNTRYMAN'S TOOLS

Garden and woodwork tools apart, the countryman will find that he needs some of the following implements from time to time.

Ax: English type, with broad head and ash shaft. For felling trees, splitting logs. In dry weather put the head in water for 20 minutes to swell the wedge and keep all tight. Hone edge with whetstone, sharpen with file.

Beet knife: Slightly curved narrow blade with a downward spike at one end and wood handle at the other. The beet is picked up by the spike and cut with the blade.

Beetle: Two handed wood mallet for driving hedgerow stakes and knocking wedges into timber. The head is of apple wood held by a forged iron band at each end, the handle of straight-grained ash tapered so that it fits tightly into the head.

Besom: A yard broom made by tightly binding a bunch of long twigs in two places near the butt end, trimming the butt with a hatchet and driving into it a pointed peeled stake as a handle.

Billhook: Broad-bladed heavy steel chopper for hedging. Will also serve for cleaving firewood.

Club hammer: For driving metal stakes into the ground or for masonry work.

Crowbar: 4-ft. steel bar, chisel-pointed at one end, crooked and notched at the other, for pulling out nails, opening cases, making holes for stakes, levering heavy stones.

Hay rake: Large wood rake with wide-spaced teeth for collecting hedge trimmings, leaves, grass.

Pickax: One end pointed, the other chisel-edged, for excavating in subsoil, clay, rock.

Rammer: Homemade from part of a tree. 3 ft. 6 in. long, 5 in. across at the base and tapering to form a handhold. For firming earth around posts and poles.

Reaping hook: Sickle like blade slightly offset from handle, for cutting grass, nettles, weeds. (A sandstone or carborundum rubber is needed for keeping the edge on reaping hook and scythe.)

Scythe: For cutting grass, harvesting corn.

Sickle: See p. 113.

● **Using a scythe.** Though hardly an implement for a child, the scythe (Fig. 4a) is less difficult to wield than its formidable blade suggests. Scythe blades come in sizes from 24 in. to 40 in., the average being about 34 in., and the wood shaft, or "snath" varies in length to suit the height of the user. The snath of the traditional scythe has a double curve which adapts well to the hand positions and body movements of the user. With practice it becomes a most efficient machine for cutting grass, coarse growth or grain, but tough tufted meadow grass is resistant to it. Besides the traditional scythe there is an admirable light scythe of Austrian manufacture called the "Turk" (Fig. 4b).

When cutting with the scythe, stand as straight

Fig. 4a
Traditional scythe

Fig. 4b
Turk scythe

as possible, your legs about 18 in. apart, left foot a little behind right. Grasp the handles or "doles" of the snath and begin the stroke with the right hand just before the right leg, then bring your right hand swiftly around to your left knee. The blade will seem to swing itself forward and then swing back for the next stroke. The art of scything is to get into and keep up a regular, rhythmic, unhurried motion, without jerkiness, not letting the blade point dig into the ground. Do not attempt too much at first. With practice your scything will improve until it becomes second nature. To sharpen the blade, wipe it over with a fistful of grass, put the butt of the snath firmly in the ground and start whetting at the base of the blade, working slowly towards the tip and holding the blade firmly by placing the left hand on top of it. To test the blade for position should the wedges loosen, hold the snath in the right working position and see that the blade is lying flat along the ground. Tighten the wedges. Carry it over the shoulder, blade at the rear.

● **Lifting sacks.** To tie a sack, pull the mouth lengthwise, stretch it and fold into pleats. Twist the twine twice around the pleated mouth and pull tight, then twist around once and pull tight again. Tie with one extra twist, and knot. In lifting a sack, first get it onto a raised platform, then back up to it and take the weight as high up on the shoulders as you can.

A heavy sack or other weight can be hoisted by means of shears (Fig. 5)—two poles lashed together near the top, then stretched apart at the bottom. The weighty object is tied to the top of the lowered shears, which are then raised by pulling on a line. A third pole can be positioned to make a tripod.

Shears making use of four lines can both raise weights and move them for a distance in a series of three operations (Fig. 6).

When heavy objects need to be hoisted, a block and tackle may be used where a suitable beam can be found to take it. A locking rope tackle can be made to lift a ton limit. By using slings, the locking rope tackle may be employed horizontally if suitable stout posts or trees are available, the slings being looped about the tree trunk and the top hook of the tackle fixed in them so that heavy objects may then be dragged across the ground, if necessary assisted by rollers and drawn by the moving block of the tackle.

A very large boulder may be moved by a long lever and the use of graded pebbles, small ones being inserted when the leverage is applied, the fulcrum being adjusted and the advantage being exploited by the insertion of larger pebbles until the boulder is rolled over, the operation being repeated. The device called the Spanish windlass, or tour-

Fig. 5

Fig. 6

niquet, is most familiar from its use to tighten the wooden frame of the fretsaw or boxsaw, but it can also be used for loosening a stubborn boulder or stump (Fig. 7). It consists of a rope with a rolling hitch and a handspike in the bight, or loop, for leverage.

For *garden tools* see p. 87 and for *woodsman's tools*, p. 65.

Fig. 7

□ 4 □

WATER SUPPLY

A country home without an adequate supply of drinking water would be no use to anybody. In areas such as the Pacific Northwest where rainfall is very heavy, water supply is not a problem. Rainwater can be caught, stored and used in the rare cases where there is no usable water belowground, so let us deal with that first.

● **Rainwater.** As 1 in. of rain will yield 3/5 gal. from each sq. ft. of roof, with a roof area of 1,000 sq. ft. and a rainfall of 35 in. per year, 21,000 gal. will be collected. Some of this will be wasted, but about 85 percent should be usable if properly stored. If a net 18,000 gal. are available for use, this works out at roughly 48 gal. a day throughout the year. Nationally, average per capita domestic water consumption is a shocking 50–100 gal. per day.

Nevertheless, 48 gal. should suffice for a small country family.

Where the house is small, the roofs of outhouses and sheds must be brought in to feed the tank, or a ground-level rain trap constructed, sloping slightly towards the tank. If the water is for drinking, all lead on the roof should be taken off and replaced by copper flashings and plastic rainwear. Slate roofs, being nonabsorbent, are better than tiles.

A storage tank will be excavated to your instructions by a contractor near one end of the house, or it can be dug by hand, using pick, shovel, bucket and wheelbarrow. Directions for making an underground cistern of 21,600 gal. (U.S.) capacity, as well as many other practical building details, are given in *A Manual on Building Construction* issued by Intermediate Technology Development Group Ltd, 25 Wilton Road, London SWıV IJS. As water is heavy, the floor of the tank must be well supported and the sides made quite watertight both to prevent leakage and to keep out impurities. The tank should be covered in and have a manhole large enough to allow it to be cleaned. A manhole with a turned-up edge, having a cover with a turned-down lip to fit over it, will keep out surface water. A circular tank is cheaper to build than a square one.

If used for drinking, rainwater should be run through a filter chamber placed between supply pipe and tank (Fig. 8). Fill the chamber with a 2- or

Fig. 8

3-ft.-sq. bed of washed gravel 1 ft. thick, on top of which is a 1½-ft. layer of fine sand. Replace the contents every year.

● **Wells.** An old country dwelling may have a well already sunk into the water-bearing stratum of the soil. It may be forgotten and invisible, covered with a stone slab, earth and grass, or its presence may be betrayed by a rusty iron pump. Uncover it and inspect the state of its brickwork or "steening," and if you are doubtful send some of the water to a public analyst for testing, meantime boiling all water before drinking it. Wells are either shallow or deep, drawing water either from the subsoil or from

a water-bearing stratum lying beneath an impermeable one, often at great depth. Shallow wells are
more likely to be polluted, especially if they are
near drains, cesspools or cattle sheds. If a well is
found to be polluted and the source is traced and
removed, it can be disinfected by adding a 5 percent chlorine solution in 1 gal. of water to each
1,200 gal. of water in the well, leaving it to stand
for 2 hours, then pumping the tainted liquid to
waste.

● **Finding water.** If there is no well or the old
well is unusable, a new well may be dug by a local
well-digger with the right equipment or by two or
three unskilled men in a few days. The driest part
of the summer should be chosen, when the water
level is low, giving a realistic idea of how much is
available, and when the soil is easier to shift. The
presence of water can be inferred from a knowledge
of local geology, but the time-honored method of
locating a water supply is through the practice of
divining by means of a dowsing wand or twig.

No special skill is needed for dowsing, though
sensitivity varies from person to person. Use a
forked piece of springy wood freshly cut from a live
tree, with arms or handles about 18 in. long and ½
in. thick. Hold the end of each handle with palms
upwards, knuckles slightly inward, the arms un-
bent and a little below the level of the hips, and

walk slowly around the area of search until the far
end of the stick dips suddenly downward, indicating water. A practiced dowser will follow an underground stream or a number of converging
streams to a blind spring known as a "head,"
where his rod will become agitated, and there give
directions for the digging of the well. These blind
springs seem to have an attraction for animals, and
dowsers claim that gnats dance always over blind
springs, that moles make their fortresses on them,
and that unconfined geese and hens always find
blind springs on which to make their nests. But
bear in mind that no dowser can tell with certainty
how deep underground is the spring he has traced,
nor can he vouch for its suitability for drinking.

● **Types of well.** An artesian well is one where
no pumping is needed to bring up the water, the
upward force being imparted by the weight of collected underground water just above the point
where the well shaft enters the natural reservoir it
taps. Such a well can be sunk on your land only if
there should happen to be a basin formed of a layer
of porous rock lying between two impermeable
layers—usually clay—the porous layer curving upwards to places at each end where it takes in moisture which then sinks through and collects at the
center of the basin. Such wells are drilled, not dug.
The specialist will have mechanical tools which can

penetrate to any depth. For depths up to 35 ft., well-boring kits can be obtained which can be worked manually. They consist of an auger made to take a number of separate cutters for use in different soils, a bailer for scooping loose sand from the bottom of the hole, and further driving tubes and connectors which can be added as depth increases. After water is struck, the borehole is sleeved with continuous pipes knocked in on top of one another. In true artesian wells the force of the water is often enough to carry it to the storage tank at the top of a building without pumping.

Underground springs can be tapped in much the same way by bores of 4–6 in. in diameter, although here the water will have to be pumped to the surface. For a very small demand, the Abyssinian tube well may meet your need. This is made up of strong tubes of light-weight steel which are driven into the soil, the bottom length perforated to let in water, having a hardened steel point for penetration of gravels and clays. As each length is knocked in, a further length is screwed or collared onto it.

● **Digging a well.** To dig a well manually, pick and shovel are needed, with a tripod of stout poles rigged up with rope, pulley and hook and a bucket for hauling up the excavated earth below shoulder level. Practiced well-diggers excavate depths of about 3 ft. at a time, timbering each section with pieces of board to prevent earth falling in. They dig several feet below the lowest level of the subsoil water, keeping the well dry meantime with continuous pumping. At the bottom they make a sump for the temporary pump by sinking a 6-in.-diameter pipe into a hole, laying around this a concrete floor. They then build up the walls from the bottom, dismantling the timbering as the walls rise. Old wells are generally brick-built, with gaps at intervals several feet up from the bottom to 'allow water to gush or seep in. If sections of concrete sleeving are used instead, the lower ones must be so arranged as to permit a similar inflow of water. Higher up, however, the brick wall will be built solid with cement mortar backed with clay to keep out surface liquids. At the top the diameter is reduced by corbelling to about 2 ft., rising not less than 1 ft. above ground level. The ground is then thickly paved or concreted, the paving sloping away from the well to a distance of at least 4 ft. in every direction. When the well is finished, the temporary pump is removed and the sump in the floor filled in, a permanent pump being now fixed in place with its suction pipe running down to the water level.

The retaining wall of the well may be of stone or of wood. Elm will last for centuries in waterlogged condition without rotting. If wood is plentiful and bricks scarce, the well shaft can be timbered— boxed-in sections placed on top of one another, the space between the wood casing and the hole being filled with gravel or graded stone rubble. Oak casks with top and bottom knocked out would seem to make a good lining, as would large steel drums of uniform size thickly coated inside and out with bituminous paint.

● **Pumps.** The primitive bucket and rope in wells was replaced by the iron pump in the last century. The mechanical pump (Fig. 9), made of wood or iron, served man for many generations. These suction pumps operate by the creation of a temporary vacuum and the emission of water through an outlet valve. Such pumps work well in shafts up to 22

Fig. 9

ft. deep, trouble arising only when the valve seating or piston becomes worn. Worn pumps need to

be primed with a pail of water before use. This type
of pump is still made. Pumps which will raise deep
water are more complicated, since the lift can no
longer be gotten by suction from a piston at ground
level; the piston must be placed at water level and
connected to the handle of the pump by reciprocat-
ing rods. The *Royale* deep-well pump, now made by
Pompes Briau, of Tours, France, is of this type and
will operate from depths up to 130 ft. H. J. Godwin
Ltd, of Quenington, Cirencester, Gloucestershire,
also make hand pumps, one of which, wheel-
operated, will lift water from 320 ft. If you have sufficient electrical power, the Sears Catalog offers
several models. Also highly recommended is the
Red Head power-driven centrifugal pump, available
from U.O.P. Johnson Division, 315 N. Pierce Street,
St. Paul, Minn. 55104

● **Springs.** A surface spring of pure water near
the house makes a well unnecessary. Deep springs
are best, their water having been thoroughly fil-
tered in its descent through soil, sand and gravel.
They are less likely to run dry in summer than surface springs. Water from such a spring on a hillside
above the house can be piped into an outdoor storage tank big enough to contain at least a week's
supply of 200 gal. While no doubt the best tanks
are of slate slabs slotted together, a useful one can
be built with concrete blocks rendered inside with

cement mortar and outside with impervious clay puddle. It must have an overflow pipe, a drainage tap and a cover. Just as satisfactory, perhaps, and quicker to erect is a modern swimming pool with rustless frame and plastic liner. From any such tank water can be brought to the house through metal, rubber or plastic tubing by means of a length of copper pipe bent into a siphon and fixed with its end some inches from the bottom of the tank. Screen the opening to keep out unwanted dirt and insects. If the spring if too low to feed the tank by gravity, the water can either be pumped up to it or pumped directly to a tank in the roof of the house.

While this could be done by an electric or wind-driven pump, the most effective engine for it is the hydraulic ram, by means of which the energy of a quantity of water with a small head is used to lift a proportionate quantity to a higher level. The way it works is that water flows from the source—a spring or a stream—along the drive pipe and through the waste valve of the ram. A waste outlet is therefore necessary. The rapid flow of water through the open waste valve causes this to shut. The momentum of water in the drive pipe then forces some of the flow through the delivery valve. This compresses the air cushion in the domed air vessel and causes a continuous outflow through the delivery pipe to the storage reservoir. If there is a sufficient fall of water, rams will work from springs giving as little as 1 gal. per minute; with a heavy rush of water, a fall of less than 3 ft. can be used, lifting water to heights of up to 400 ft. Rams are trouble-free, cost nothing to run, last indefinitely and are relatively cheap.

● **Modern plumbing** is so laborsaving that it would be shortsighted not to install it in a dwelling where it is lacking. The amateur can manipulate some modern materials without plumbing skill. Heavy-duty polythene or alkathene tubes, which can be cut with knife or saw, have thick enough walls to allow connection by special screwed or compression fittings. Begin by fitting a tank under the roof, with a ball valve and waste pipe and an outlet to supply the pipes running to the bathroom and kitchen. Polythene is elastic and will expand without bursting in a breeze and thaw, and is especially suitable for cold water supply. But as it has a melting point of only 225–235° F it is not suitable for hot water.

□ 5 □

GARBAGE AND SEWAGE DISPOSAL, SANITATION

In a properly managed country household the disposal of garbage presents no problems, most of the waste being returned to the soil either indirectly through animals or directly through composting. There should be four lidded bins for the main types of refuse: (1) food scraps, (2) vegetable waste, (3) metal, glass and plastic trash and (4) paper. Of these, (1) and (2) will be emptied daily, (3) and (4) when full. (1) can be fed in a mash to pigs or poultry. Otherwise the scraps can be composted. To avoid attracting rats, cover with earth and sprinkle with chloride of lime, or use a patented compost bin such as the Sears Rotocrop Accelerator. (2) can be thrown straight onto the compost heap; (3) must be buried in a pit which can be earthed over when full, all metal cans being first crushed flat; (4) can be burned on the kitchen stove or in a garden incinerator. This may be of the heavy brazier type on legs—avoid flimsy wire baskets which burn out and corrode—or it can be built up with loose bricks and a metal grid having a space beneath for ash removal. This will burn not only uncompostable paper but any organic material too dense to be rotted down.

● **Drains.** Until recently old cottages and farmhouses had no plumbing or sewage systems, the kitchen water in a bucket or bowl being flung out of the back door onto the garden, and baths carried out and tipped into a ditch. Rather than let waste water escape from the house to run on the soil surface, dig a trench not less than 1 ft. deep and with a fall of about ⅛ inch in the foot through towards the end of the garden, line it with medium-sized stones, gravel and ash and place on top a line of agricultural drain pipes loosely butted together, with a sump or sink at the far end, and near to the house a grid to strain off large particles which might clog the pipes. Such a drain might be laid in part beneath a garden path and run towards a flanking ditch.

● **Disposal of excrement.** By and large, city-bred people have come to consider their own body wastes as so much filth which must be gotten out of sight and mind as secretly and completely as possible. The result is that many who come to live in a cottage think only of installing a town-type bathroom with an outlet, preferably to a main sewer or to a small-scale sewage system (cesspool or septic tank), with all the expense and waste of space this involves.

Such people have to extricate themselves from their early conditioning and learn afresh that human excrement or shit is nothing more than the unusable part of quite wholesome substances taken into the digestive system as food, processed and ejected by it as waste organic material. This waste when naturally decomposed may be brought back into the cycle of life as plant nutrients in the same way as any other animal dung. It is only when the organism is diseased that excreta may carry infection through rats and flies. The simplest and most satisfactory method of disposal is to add this waste to the compost heap and cover it with a shovelful of earth to keep off the flies. Here it will rapidly lose its noisome qualities and aid the decomposition of the other matter. In this way a valuable manure is conserved instead of being foolishly thrown away. Urine, too, contains nitrogens, phosphates and sulphates which can feed plants. The following disposal methods are set out in order of preference from the point of view of the conservation of the fertilizing properties of excrement.

A **privy,** placed just outside the back door or further afield, may have either a fixed or a movable receptacle with some means for the automatic strewing of dry, loamy earth after use. This may be held in a box over the seat, feeding through a hopper to a chute ending just above the bucket or tank at the back, with a flap to govern its flow; or it may be caused to fall down by the weight of the user on the seat. If a fixed tank is used, it should be one that can be emptied from the rear of the privy; if a bucket, the seat must lift up to let it be carried away and emptied. Either tank or bucket when new should be treated inside with a coat of tar, which will prolong its life and make it easier to empty. The work of emptying bucket or tank is the only drawback to this perfectly hygienic system.

Such work can be cut down a bit, and a concession made to city-bred prejudice, by using instead a **chemical privy** which incorporates a ventilation chamber through which an air draft carries fumes to an outlet pipe behind the seat, and an inner container into which a chemical preparation diluted with water is poured before it is brought into use. This quells the stink and reduces the bulk of the excreta without destroying its value as fertilizer. Also available are powdered chemicals which, when sprinkled over the contents of the bucket, foster the growth of minute fungi which feed on them and reduce their bulk. This system ends with matter which can be used as an activator on compost heaps and is viable so long as supplies of the chemical are assured.

There is now on the market the **Clivus Multrum,** a Swedish plastic-walled latrine-cum-compost heap in which aerobic action is used to digest the excreta, which are dropped without either water or earth into a ventilated chamber with a sloping floor directly beneath the seat, where they slide down a 16-degree slope to a second chamber which is fitted with a lid for the tipping of kitchen and garden waste, and with perforated iron pipes to let in air. The mixture heats up and decomposes and then slides gradually under a partition into the third and largest chamber, from which it is removed and used in the garden. It is an ingenious and laborsaving system, but the cost and cumbersomeness of the structure must be weighed against the work it saves; for after all it does nothing which cannot be done just as well with a privy and a compost heap. However, it would seem preferable to a septic tank should the local sanitation authority accept it as an alternative, while insisting on either one or the other. Check local or regional farming and homesteading magazines for sales and installation in your area.

The same effect as the Swedish system at less cost can be gained by simple **composting in a privy pit.** For this one must have a transportable shed-type privy with door, seat and (for daytime lighting) a transparent vinyl roof. This is sited on a pair of reinforced concrete slabs laid over a fairly deep pit. Pit privies, properly made and maintained, are recognized as one of the safest sewage disposal methods. A pit vent can be installed, extending above the roof; the seat should be cut out of a board which can then be hinged backward to allow kitchen and garden waste to be thrown into the pit.

Having dug your pit and made sure that its base is above the groundwater level (place it so that runoff water will not flow through it), cover the bottom 2 ft. with lawn mowings, leaves and straw. Over the top of the pit place the slabs, leaving a gap in the middle for fall of excreta and rubbish. Tip all household and garden garbage into the pit and add wood ash, cut grass and slaked lime with some earth once a week. When the contents are a foot or so from the surface, move slabs and privy to a new pit not less than 6 ft. away. Level the first pit with 6 in. of grass and leaves and fill in with firmly rammed earth. When the second pit is filled, the compost in the first will be ready for removal to the garden. Use a long-handled dung fork to get it out. The pit can then be used again.

Both cesspools and septic tanks are wasteful and expensive methods of sewage disposal, but of the two the septic tank is much to be preferred. **Cesspools** have nothing to recommend them except that, like septic tanks, they permit the use of indoor toilets. Cesspools, which are forbidden in many areas and, where permitted, regulated as to size, depth and location, are simply large storage containers in which sewage collects until it can be emptied, usually by a professional service with vacuum-operated tankers. What if this service breaks down? They become quite uneconomical when water from baths and sinks is run into them; and defective ones can be a source of soil contamination and water pollution.

The **septic tank** by contrast is really a miniature municipal sewage farm, more appropriate for the large country house than the humble cottage. Septic tanks must usually have a 750-1,000-gal. capacity and must otherwise comply with local building and sanitary codes. All kitchen and bathroom wastes run through underground pipes to a distant brick-built settling tank on a concrete base. Here the solids in the waste are digested by anaerobic bacteria, during which process they give off methane or marsh gas into the atmosphere. When the fluid in this tank reaches a high enough level it floods over into a second, smaller tank from which it runs into a shallow filter bed made of brickwork on a concrete base, and having a bed of clinker or coke. The effluent is spread over it either by perforated iron pipes or corrugated asbestos sheets placed at a slight slope and punctured with holes through which the fluid drips. Here aerobic activity breaks down the effluent to its final state, when it drips through an outlet pipe at the end of the system and is either discharged into a ditch or stream or made to run through land drains into the soil. You should tip no disinfectant into such a system for fear of killing the bacteria on which its functioning depends.

If the settling tank is made airtight and the methane gas it generates drawn off into a small-scale expanding gasometer and from there piped to the kitchen, it can be used to fuel a stove. In this case, insulation of the tank in winter is called for, and maybe some gentle heating—in both cases to keep up the 85-90° F of warmth necessary for the multiplying bacteria. Further information on this type of arrangement can be obtained from *The Mother Earth News* by writing for Mother's Methane Package, P.O. Box 70, Hendersonville, NC 28739.

Part II:

MORE ESSENTIAL AMENITIES

□ 6 □

WOOD FIRES
AND STOVES

Quite often, old farmhouses and cottages have
fairly modern fireplaces which, if removed, reveal
that an old-fashioned iron range or suchlike has
once stood there, the original open chimneypiece
having been bricked in to take it. These bricks can
be knocked away to expose the original hearth and
wide chimney of the preindustrial hearth with its
damper, its great breastbeam and chimney corners.
There is then a choice—to keep the original hearth
and burn logs, or to install a closed stove which
will burn not only wood but peat, anthracite, coke
and coal. Before deciding, survey the likely future
fuel supplies in the neighborhood. If there is an
abundant supply of cheap or free wood, there is
much to be said for an open hearth, even though
much of the heat from it goes up the chimney.

There should be a large solid hearthstone a few
inches above the floor, an iron fireback and

andirons across which to lay the logs. Logs may be 3–4 ft. long and 4–6 in. thick, for the longer the logs your fire will take, the less labor there is in cutting them. One large, heavy log at the back of the fire, propped by stones or held by a chain to keep it from rolling into the flame, will produce a slow, steady heat for weeks before it is consumed. As the wood burns, leave the ashes to gather on the hearthstone for a week or more. They will keep the heat all night. The fire will die right down to embers, but these have only to be scattered with shavings and light branches in the morning and gently breathed upon with the bellows and they will spring to life, so that a good fire may be had very quickly. If a glowing stick or log is buried under a pile of ash in the hearth, next morning it will still be alight and can be blown into a flame.

If coal is to be burned on an open fire it is better to have a modern fireplace with a clay fireback which throws heat into the room. Never use coal on a wood fire, for the ash and clinker of even a few coals destroy the purity of a wood fire. Peat can be used, but if peat and wood are burned together a hard deposit may form in the chimney which is difficult to remove.

● **Iron stoves.** But you may not have such a hearth and chimney, and the kitchen and hall to go with them. You may have one large living room which you want to heat, by wood, as cheaply as possible. An enclosed iron stove with a top opening for a metal chimney may meet your needs. The Franklin company makes several types of these, some of which take quite long logs and burn for long periods without refueling. Jøtul, a Norwegian company also makes such stoves and markets them in the United States through local distributors.

If you want a modern stove which will cook your food, heat your water and warm the room as well, there is a model called the AFS Fireplace Wood Burning Stove which also takes coal, paper and "buffalo chips." The Sears catalogue features four wood-burning heaters, one of which also uses coal and two of which can double as cook stoves. There are instructions for making your own wood stove from old water-heater tanks in *The Mother Earth News*, No. 49, January–February 1978. You can also consult *The Wood Burning Stove Book* by Geri Harrington (1977) and *Wood Stoves: How to Make and Use Them* by Ole Wik (1977).

● **Kindling a fire.** In the absence of paper perhaps the best kindling for a fire is the finely shredded bark of the birch tree, which is oily and burns with a smoky flame like a candle. It would be a thrifty practice to strip any birch logs you have of their bark and keep this for kindling. From the garden, dried sunflower and artichoke stalks make good kindling. Fir cones can be collected in sacks by children and used to start the fire. Among unusual fuels are the otherwise useless timbers from demolished buildings: when sawing these, beware of hidden nails which can badly damage the saw blade. The sea yields driftwood daily in rough weather, and in some areas sea coal. For charcoal and peat, see Sections 8 and 9. When lighting a peat fire, remember that it will not catch from paper only but needs a basis of wood kindling. Large unbroken turfs should not be put on to a newly lighted fire—they will put it out. Instead, break them up between the fingers and feed the fire with them gradually, giving it your whole attention for the first 10 minutes. When the fire has taken hold, pile the hearth up with large sods; if they appear to quell the blaze, it will soon shoot up again. A peat fire will call for more use of the bellows than a wood or coal fire. As peat is bulkier than coal in relation to the time it takes to burn, it needs larger containers than the normal coal scuttle. Though it requires more attention while burning, peat makes less dirt than coal and has a pleasant fragrance. Stack the peats closely at night and they will be found still glowing at the center next morning.

□ 7 □

GETTING WOOD
FOR FUEL

The modern tool for felling trees and cutting up logs is the portable chain saw. This is a ferocious implement consisting of a small gasoline engine held within the frame of the saw and operating a band or chain with teeth which chew into the wood. The noise, weight and vibration are compensated by the saw's capacity for cutting through logs like cheese, reducing a huge tree to manageable balks of timber in an incredibly short time. Many farmers now have one of these things. If a large tree near your house is blown down and you wish to have the wood for fuel, you could perhaps hire or borrow a chain saw. It is hardly worthwhile buying one.

The ordinary tools required for wood cutting in the open, felling trees, removing branches live and dead and cutting hedges back are: a tubular-frame coarse-toothed bow saw with a blade that is secured with a wing nut; a hatchet, an ax and a bill-hook. You may also need a sledge hammer and two or three iron wedges. For bringing down large trees a cross cut saw worked by two men is needed; but the beginning woodsman should attempt only trees of moderate size—say not more than 30 feet high and 1 foot in diameter at the base.

● **Felling a tree.**   An experienced woodsman will fell a large tree by making the cut as near to the ground as possible. The first stage is called laying in, when the buttresses or swellings leading to the roots are sheared off with an ax. This done, a tapering gap is made on the face of the trunk—the part facing the way the tree is to fall—taking away the support on that side. The ax is now put aside, and two men take up the cross cut saw and begin to cut on the back of the tree. All the work of a cross cut is done on the pull stroke, each man in turn pulling and releasing, or following through the other's pull. Until a hundred years ago trees were normally felled with the ax alone. In that case, after the first opening was made on the face as described, the second opening on the back was made somewhat higher, causing the tree to go down more readily. Felling is always done in the winter months after Christmas. No one would wish to fell a tree when its sap was rising or it was in full leaf.

Suppose you wish to take down a tree of moderate size. You will notice first whether there is enough space for it to fall in the direction towards which it leans and towards which the height of its top branches inclines it to sway. Hew out a wide notch with the ax, on the back of the tree and as low as is practicable. Putting the ax aside, continue cutting with the cross cut saw, but stop as soon as there are signs of movement in the tree. Take out the saw and tap one or two iron wedges into the cut, using a sledge hammer or the heel of the ax. With a little skill you can direct in this way where the tree is to lie when it falls. A less deft way is to fasten a rope to the tree at about three quarters of its height before cutting begins, the rope being long enough to pass well beyond the point where the top of the tree will strike the ground. When the tree begins to topple, get your helpers to pull together in the right direction on the rope while you drive the wedges home. Once fallen—and do avoid letting the tree fall so that it leans propped up against another tree—the limbs can be sheared off with ax and saw and the trunk cut into movable sections with the cross cut. Keep out of the way of suddenly falling limbs and the crushing weight of the trunk when it rolls off balance as a heavy limb is removed.

● **To remove side branches** from a growing tree so placed that it is not convenient to let them drop to the ground, dismember them piecemeal, sawing through branches one by one and lowering them by a rope. The rope, which should have a heavy iron hook spliced into one end, may be of good manila or nylon of ¾-in. diameter and in length rather more than twice the height of the uppermost bough to be taken off. Begin, though, with the lowest bough. Climb the tree, fix the rope at the point of balance by passing it around the branch and catching it in the hook. Pass the other free end of the rope over a branch or fork a few feet higher up the tree. Bring the free end of the rope to the ground and let a helper secure it by taking a turn of it around the trunk and holding on to the end, making sure there is no slackness in the operational part of the rope. Then begin sawing the branch with your bow saw, first cutting an inch or two upwards on the lower side, and then almost all the way through from above. If the rope is kept taut you need not fear the branch will suddenly break away. When the saw is through except for the last ½ in., get off the tree and gradually ease off the turn of the rope round the trunk. The limb will crack and come away, and may be safely lowered. If you have no helper then make the bight of the rope fast with a hitch while you are up the tree.

● **Sawing logs.** To convert tree timber into fuel you will need a rough horse to hold the balk of timber while it is being sawed. This is a strong, heavy frame of rough timber, made by constructing two wooden X's and joining them at about 3 ft. apart by stout struts and crosspieces. The bottom part of the X makes the feet while the top part holds the log to be sawed, the bottom part being larger than the top for stability.

The work of sawing is halved if two people saw the logs using the cross cut. As with felling a tree the knack is to keep the saw running smoothly to and fro along its whole length every stroke without jamming or bending—keep it perfectly straight. When sawing very large pieces, tap a wedge into the cut into which the saw is disappearing, knocking it a little further in as sawing proceeds. Keep an oil can handy, as a few drops on the saw now and then will ease its way through resistant wood. After use, brush all sawdust out of the teeth of the cross cut and rub it over with an oily rag.

● **Chopping billets.** If the sawed pieces are too big for the stove, they must be split on the chopping block, the stump of a tree about 3 ft. high and 2 ft. across standing solid on the ground. Upend the billet on the block and bring down the ax with a sharp blow near its center. It should split instantaneously. The straighter the grain of the wood, the less force is needed for the blow: straight-grained wood splits by itself, fibrous woods like fir and oak need more force, while cross-grained timber may defy the ax, yielding only to wedges driven in by repeated blows of the sledge.

Logs will stand the weather if stacked on their sides in the open but will burn better if kept dry. They may be protected with tarpaulin, plastic sacks, corrugated iron or old linoleum. Billets and cleft wood need to be kept under cover in a fuel store; if there is room enough to house the tools and horse also, wood can be chopped and sawed on wet days.

● **Twigs.** The old woodsmen wasted no part of the tree, and where the modern chain-saw man will too often burn the mountain of small branches left after his operations, leaving a charred circle in the soil, they would lay them together in long bunches and bind them tightly with withes or wire, in this way making them into combustible branches. Similarly, when hedges were cut, the wood was separated into three piles, for pea sticks, for bean poles, and bind the leavings into branches. These were burned whole in the tunnel of the cottage bread-oven. Chopped with the bill on the block into short lengths, they can also be used for kindling. They can be stored in the open in a large pile with the bundles laid length wise on the top and sloping like a roof.

Twigs can also be used for the floor of the calf or goat pen, with straw litter on top: the straw keeps cleaner this way as the animals' urine passes through it and drains away through the twigs.

● **Tree roots.** Stumps may be grubbed up by a tractor with a set of chains, or by a hand-operated monkey, an engine fitted with a low-geared winch worked by a lever which enables one man to pull the stump slowly out of the ground with some of its roots attached. To do this, attach the cable securely to the stump and fasten the other end to a stump or a standing tree trunk. When working the winch, you stand with your back to the stump to be pulled out. If you are faced with large numbers of tree stumps, it may be quicker to blast them out with explosives. Tree stumps, having twisted and distorted fibers, are difficult to split or saw and may be burned on the site.

● **Splitting a tree trunk.** One sometimes comes up against a long, heavy trunk which can neither be moved nor easily sawed. Sometimes such trunks can be split open along the grain of the wood, using a heavy sledge, three or four iron wedges, and half a dozen larger beechwood wedges for keeping the gap open once it is made. This works better with ash, beech, oak and the softwoods than with elm. Use a crowbar for levering open the split at the last stage. Having split such a trunk, you have two or more lengthy balks of timber which can either be sawed into handy sections or hauled away as they are.

Most timber from full-grown trees is too valuable for fuel. Remember that your fallen tree might fetch a good price from a timber merchant before you begin cutting it to pieces. Wood sold for burning is usually branchwood or coppice stems, the heat potential of which depends on how long it has been seasoned. It is best to buy the winter's store in the previous spring and allow it to season in the open throughout the summer, preferably under an open shelter. When buying, remember too that unseasoned wood, since it contains more moisture, is heavier than seasoned: so if the price is the same, buy the seasoned.

□8□

CHARCOAL

Before coal was extensively mined, charcoal for domestic and light industrial use was produced by the burning of logs at their place of growth, the forests, in such a way that the charred remnants could be the more easily carried away and stored for fuel. Charcoal is very light in weight, and yet it is almost the perfect fuel, as it yields steady high temperatures without smoke or ash. One hundred parts of wood yield about 60 parts by measure, or 25 parts by weight, of charcoal. So 1 ton of green timber will give about 20 bushels, or 400 lb., of charcoal. Its domestic use today is as a starter for anthracite stoves; but a charcoal stove can be used indoors not only to grill meat and fish but to bake scones, roast potatoes and boil vegetables and stews.

Charcoal is produced by heating wood in the absence of sufficient air for complete combustion.

The heat first drives out the water from the wood, then the volatile compounds including creosote and tar, leaving the lightweight solids: black carbon with some mineral ash. Almost any wood will make charcoal, chestnut and coppice oak being considered best. No special tools are needed; the rough wood is just cut into lengths of 2–4 ft. and stacked for several months to season. Burning is done in the summer.

Charcoal is now made commercially in sealed metal furnaces from which the liquid by-products are run off for use. This suggests the possibility, which might bear investigation, of burning charcoal in discarded oil drums in which the draft could be easily controlled. Fluids could be left to drain off through holes drilled in the base of the drum, which would be raised above ground level on breeze blocks, and piped or channeled into small tins or drums.

□9□

PEAT

Those cottagers who have access to it may well consider using peat, for centuries the most widespread household fuel in Ireland and Scotland. Large deposits of peat are found in Michigan, California and the Florida Everglades.

Peat consists of partly rotted vegetable matter and not, like coal, of extinct varieties of lycopodiaceous trees compressed and chemically altered into hard carbon. The conditions for its formation are the presence of water and decaying vegetation and the scarcity of oxygen. It is said to take 100 years to form a 6-ft. depth of peat, and the depth of a bed may vary from 2 to 20 ft. The best slow-burning peat is coal black in color, the poorer type a light brown. The time for cutting is in April or May, for it must have a full summer to dry out before it can be used the following winter. If carting is difficult it may be left until later when the bog surface is dryer.

● **Cutting peat.** First, the top layer of grass and soil is stripped off to get at the peat bed itself, using a broad-bladed spade, with an old scythe blade or hay knife to cut into the rough herbage. Next the peat itself is cut, customarily with a special spade with a foot-long blade 6 in. across, along one edge of which another spur-shaped blade, the "feather," is set at right angles, so that it will cut out an oblong block of peat in one operation. A block should be about 12–18 in. long and from 4–6 in. wide, by about the same thickness.

Peat cutting is best done with a gang or a pair, one to cut, the others to stack, since wet peat is heavy. Cut at a vertical face extending through the peat bed to the mineral soil beneath, unless the bed is a very deep one. Take the face steadily backwards as the work goes on until the whole bed is worked out.

If the peats are not to be dried on the spot, they are carried to a drying ground and there spread out singly. They are turned after a few days so that both sides dry evenly. Later they are turned again and stacked on their ends, leaning together like little wigwams. This lets them dry out in the wind, this drying being completed later in larger openwork stacks. As peats dry out they shrink and lose weight; a ton of fresh-cut peat makes only 300–400 lb. of dry fuel. When dry they are carted to the house and stored under cover or in close stacks with sloping sides to shed the rain.

□10□

OIL LAMPS
AND CANDLES

Although convenient, electric lighting utterly destroys the poetic apprehension of the difference between night and day and resembles flame lighting about as much as the electric fire resembles the fire of wood, peat or coal. The old-time pioneer lit his home in winter with tallow candles, or with rushlights made by stripping all the skin except a narrow vertical ribbon from the pith of a meadowrush and soaking it in a dish of melted fat. The dried rushlight was nipped between a pair of metal pincers on an iron stand and shifted forward from time to time as it burned down. Cobbett preferred these to candles, largely because they were cheaper.

Paraffin lamps later became popular because the oil was cheap, and because its volatile nature allowed it to ascend a wick by capillary action and to be present for burning at the wick top where it would vaporize fairly easily. Fish and vegetable oils were inferior in these respects. The lightest of these, colza or rapeseed oil, needed a lamp with a gravity-feed system with a separate raised reservoir and a complex of valves and vents to get the oil where it was wanted and to drain away overflow. Without such a machine, such oils can be burned only in the simplest lamps of all, the ancient cruses, with or without spouts and lids, where the burning point of the wick is in direct contact with the fuel, and which give only a feeble light. In the early years of the century the houses of the well-to-do were sometimes lit by acetylene gas produced by the action of water on carbide of calcium, which produced a brilliant white light. Carbide today is unobtainable in the shops, and will burn only in specially made, outmoded lamps. The same goes for air gas, a mixture of air with a small amount of gasoline vapor.

This leaves us today with propane, which can be fed from large cylinders through a system of supply pipes, or from a small cylinder connected to a single lamp; it is effective but is more economical for heating and cooking than for lighting.

In the absence of electricity the country dweller must depend either upon propane or upon the **paraffin lamp** for night lighting. The most efficient hanging or table lamps are of the Aladdin type, which have an incandescent mantle of asbestos fiber suspended on a wire frame above a circular wick, the whole being mounted upon the oil reservoir and enclosed by a glass chimney. The soft 100-watt light can be improved by slipping a second glass chimney over the first. If the wick is turned too high the mantle will slowly blacken with soot: rectify by turning the wick low so that the charcoal on mantle and chimney are burned away. If a little fine salt is sprinkled down the glass the mantle will clear itself more quickly.

The Tilley type pressure lamp is really a safety storm lantern. It burns with a hissing noise and can be used indoors or out. It has a mantle which grips the top of a central burner stem up which the oil is forced by air pressure from a pump set obliquely into the reservoir. Before it will light, the mantle and stem have to be preheated with methylated spirit. When the oil reaches the burner at the top of the stem it is vaporized and turns into inflammable gas. The lamp slowly loses pressure and has to be pumped up; there is also some tendency for air to leak out at the points where stem and pump enter the reservoir. The owner of either type of lamp should have a reserve of spare mantles, chimneys, special wicks (Aladdin), and washers and springs (Tilley), none of which can be improvised.

The simplest, most reliable but least efficient oil lamp is the standard flat-wick burner, consisting of reservoir, single or double wick, winding mechanism and chimney. Its outdoor counterpart is the tinned metal storm lantern. Spare wicks and chimneys only are needed.

● **Candles** give more light than simple cruses. The best are of beeswax, the next best of paraffin wax, the worst of tallow, which is any kind of hard animal fat. Tallow must first be rendered in boiling water; the fat floats to the top and is skimmed off, leaving the cellular fabric behind. Beeswax may be bought from a beekeeper, paraffin wax from a hardware store. Candles can be made in molds such as the casing of a bicycle pump sawed through lengthwise, or a disposable plastic container which, if used only once, need not be cut in two. A rustic mold is a length of dried cow-parsley stalk cut between the "knuckles." Insert a length of string for wick, and center it by tying each end to the middle of a nail or matchstick resting upon top and bottom of the mold. Bind the two parts of the mold together and fix in an upright position. Pour in melted wax or salt-free tallow at the top end. Allow to harden, and add more wax as needed. Unbind the mold, dip it in hot water and take out the cold candle. Make and store a quantity of candles, as they harden and improve with age. In the absence of suitable molds, make a cylindrical impression in a pile of wet sand and fasten the bottom end of the wick to a metal or stone weight. The thicker the candle the thicker in proportion must be the wick: an old bootlace makes a good wick for a thick candle. Dip all wicks in boric acid to make them burn brighter. Lighted candles need to be trimmed now and then by the nipping off of a charred piece of the burning wick. As well as being pushed into a bottle or candlestick—first dipping the base of the candle in hot water—a candle may be spiked on an upturned nail.

Part III:

GARDENING FOR SURVIVAL

□11□

THE VEGETABLE GARDEN

● **Making the garden.** Sometimes the new occupant of a country house inherits a well-made garden, but he is as likely to find a neglected area overgrown with rank weeds, a patch of virgin grassland or a waste plot covered with rusty stoves and bicycle frames, bottles and cans. If he is fortunate the garden will have a southerly aspect, will be protected from winds and be unshaded by trees.

Grassland is easiest to deal with. Strip the turf from the soil with mattock or spade and pile it in heaps, grass side down, to rot into friable humus. If the garden is a rubbish dump, the bricks and large stones must be wheeled away and stacked in piles from which they can later be retrieved for making paths or drain channels, while broken bed frames, bottles and cans must be buried. (Some of these metal objects can be used later when reinforced concrete is wanted.) Metal containers may be crushed flat, but glass bottles should be left whole and buried bottom up in sand or ash in the pathways.

Neglected gardens or virgin land can be turned over to two or more pigs for cleaning and plowing. The plot must be well fenced—a two-strand electric fence will do—and there must be clean water for the pigs to drink and simple huts for shelter. A pig house can be made from straw bales or from two sheets of corrugated iron fastened along the top and spread open at the bottom, or from thatched hurdles. If grass and weeds are high they should first be scythed, raked and stacked in a corner to rot. Brambles should be cut and burned. Scatter the pigs' rations, in the form of cubes, over the plot. In a year a couple of pigs will convert a half-acre wilderness into a plowed, weeded and dunged area which needs only to be hand-harrowed to be ready for planting.

The question of gardening without digging will be dealt with later, but it should be noted here that it is possible to start gardening on grassland by planting potatoes on the grass and then covering them with damp straw to the depth of 1 ft; the grass will rot down to nutrient matter on which the potatoes will feed.* The straw can be moved the following season and a crop of peas and beans sown where the potatoes were.

* See W. E. Shewell-Cooper, *The Complete Vegetable Grower* (London: Faber, 1974) p. 87.

Without pigs or straw, the garden will have to be plowed or dug. Grass and annual weeds are no trouble, but perennial growth like couch grass, thistles and coltsfoot may be a nuisance. Farmers have found that couch grass (twitch) will disintegrate if plowed under every month from March to September, when it will restore to the soil as much plant food as a crop of mustard grown for green manure. Thistles and coltsfoot can be banished in the same way, by plowing or digging. Some obdurate weeds, like docks, will have to be grubbed out and thrown on the compost heap after being dried in the sun or crushed to pulp.

● **Garden tools.** With few exceptions the best tools are the traditional ones. Good tools may sometimes be picked up very cheaply at country auction sales, where they are often sold in assorted bundles. Buy two or three such bundles, select the tools which suit you, tie up the rest and put them back for sale. If you buy new never let the price of a really good tool deter you. It is wasted money to buy inferior tools. Don't buy on sight but try out every tool for balance, and put down your money only when you are sure that it is right for you.

You will need:

1. *Garden spade.* For rough digging and excavating. The spade should balance well and have a spring-

tempered, all-steel blade (not stainless) with a tread on the top edge to protect your instep. Clean the blade after use with a piece of slate or shaped hardwood. Rub down all tool handles once a year with linseed oil. Wipe blades with an oily rag.

2. *Garden fork.* A four-tined fork is needed for breaking up dug ground, lifting roots, etc. A flat-tined potato-lifting fork and a round-tined dung fork are also useful.

3. *Mattock.* An invaluable tool, being a steel blade like a long, heavy hoe set at right angles to a handle of shaped ash. The blade needs to be about 9 in. long by 6 in. wide, and the handle stout in proportion. Use with a swinging movement for taking out trenches for potato planting, for slicing turf from new ground, for rough digging and heavy hoeing.

4. *Manure hook* (Fig. 10). A blacksmith can make one by bending the tines of a garden fork at right angles to the shaft and replacing the fork handle with a 5-ft. ash pole. Used for mucking out sheds, this is a useful tool for breaking up the soil to a depth of 4 or 5 in. in "no-digging" gardening.

5. *Hand hoe.* You need two hoes, a Dutch hoe, or scuffle hoe, with a flat head that is pushed to cut down weeds just below soil level, and a Warren hoe with a swan neck used to single out seedlings or to draw soil around the stems of plants.

6. *Garden rake.* Get one with a long handle and ten

teeth, with teeth and neck forged in one piece. Don't use broomsticks as hoe or rake handles.

7. *Hand trowel.* For digging up small plants, potting, transplanting. If it is just 1 ft. long it will serve for measuring distances between plants and rows. A hand fork is also useful.

Fig. 10

8. *Hand harrow* or *cultivator.* Has three or five spear-point prongs curved like grapnels at the end of a long straight handle. Choose one with fixed prongs. (In general, avoid all composite and multi-purpose tools and those with interchangeable parts.)

9. *Dibble.* A shortened fork handle ending in a steel-shod point for making holes for leeks, potatoes, onion sets, cabbages.

10. *Wheelbarrow.* A big, rugged barrow with strong legs set wide apart, bought from a builders' supplier, for carting earth, muck and compost, potatoes, etc.

11. *Seed drill* and *garden line.* The line, tied at each end to an 18-in. stake, must be as long as the widest part of your garden plot. It is used as a

guide to the draw hoe when it makes the drill for seed sowing, the earth being filled in afterwards with the rake and firmed with the rake head or by tramping. But the best way to sow seed is to use a seed drill having a seed hopper with release mechanism geared to a wheel which runs along the ground and a variable arm which enables the user to keep the wheel at the required distance from the previous row.

12. *Other tools.* A 1½-gal. or 2-gal. watering can with screwed-on rose. A plastic or rubber garden hose on a reel. A long-handled spade without the usual handgrip reduces bending: used to sling earth from one spot to another. A roadman's shovel for sand and gravel, and a riddle, or sieve, for separating fine soil, etc., from coarse. Some shallow wooden boxes for seed trays; flower pots; some rows of glass or plastic cloches. A caveat: Don't garden in shoes to which wet soil readily adheres, but wear thick-soled leather boots.

● **Planning the garden.** We shall not be concerned here with the ornamental but solely with the practical aspects of gardening, the growing of vegetables and fruits for food. Let us assume that your garden is south-facing or that it gets enough sunshine throughout the day, that it is not overshaded, that the soil is reasonably fertile and easy to work, and that it is large enough to grow the vegetables

you require throughout the year. How big is "large enough"? It has been estimated that a garden of ⅛ acre (= 605 sq. yd. i.e. one 60 yd. long by 10 yd. wide, or 30 yd. long by 20 yd. wide) will provide all the vegetables needed by a family of four, without the luxuries, and including potatoes; and that such a garden would take 288 man-hours a year to work properly—on average, less than an hour a day.*
With a garden twice as large, and with less than twice as much work, one would be able to plant fruit bushes, some apple and pear trees and a strawberry bed; and with anything much larger there would be scope for growing a patch of cereals for home use, and food for stock or for sale.

Just as simple gardening can be done with only a spade, fork, rake and hoe, so it can be done without a planned garden, and without the shed, greenhouse, frame and hotbed that advanced gardeners find so necessary. But it is always best to think ahead from the beginning even with the roughest garden and the scantiest equipment, and to plan the garden for the easy working of a four-course rotation system by dividing it into four main plots for this purpose, with a further plot for such permanent crops as rhubarb, asparagus, cucumbers, summer squashes and perhaps Jerusalem artichokes (Table 1).

The purpose of rotation is to give the land 3 years to recover from the food demands of a particular

* Shewell-Cooper, op. cit., p. 20.

Table 1 ROTATION OF CROPS

Assuming the garden to be rectangular, divide it into five plots of a size to be governed by the quantities of the various vegetables it is intended to grow. The fifth section is set aside for perennial and secondary crops, the other four for crop rotation, the plan repeating itself every four years.

Plot 1	Plot 2	Plot 3	Plot 4
Beans, peas, celery	Beet, carrots, parsnips	Cabbage, broccoli, savoy, sprouts, cauliflower, turnips, onions, leeks, shallots, lettuces, spinach	Potatoes
(move to next plot the following year)	→	→	→

Plot 5
Asparagus, horseradish, rhubarb, sea kale, herbs, artichokes, mustard and cress, etc. Bush fruits: currants, gooseberries, raspberries. Strawberry bed (move every 3 years). Seedbed for raising brassicas.

type of crop while allowing that crop in the following year to avoid whatever pests or disease spores peculiar to itself have been left behind in the soil, and by which the successor crop in the rotation will be unaffected. At the same time it allows a system of manuring to be carried out, a large quantity of organic manure always being given to the plot planted with potatoes, and slaked lime at the rate of 1–2 lb. per sq. yd. to the next plot before it is sown with legumes. The legumes then hand over to the following crop the nitrogen they have fixed in their roots.

A four-plot garden with a further fixed plot at the far end is obviously best approached from a path down the middle, with perhaps another path running across at right angles. Any lawn will be near the house, perhaps separated from it by a paved area serving in summer as an outside room. Place the herb garden near the kitchen door. Tool shed, potting and storage sheds, if you have them, should be concealed by a hedge or by a row of sunflowers or artichokes at the near end of the garden, as should the cold frame and greenhouse, if any. Cultivate right up to the edge of the garden, leaving no grassy, weedy border. Make paths hard enough to take a loaded barrow without crumbling. Also essential is a path to the clothes line, so decide where that is to be fixed and make a path to it which will keep your feet dry at all seasons. Wherever the compost heap is to be, it will need a strong concrete track running up to it. Minor paths may be of gravel or cinders or concrete slabs, and a path across a lawn is best made of spaced stepping-stones sunk level with the ground so that they do not obstruct scythe or mower.

● **Fruit.** If the garden is large enough, grow fruit on a permanent site at its far end. If there is room for the planting of a small orchard, grass it down, and pigs, geese or hens can be run on it without harm to the trees. The beginner will find that less skill in pruning and training is required to grow apples and pears as bushes or standard or half-standard trees than as espaliers, fans, etc. Make sure that if the varieties chosen are not self-fertile they are paired with the right cross-pollinating variety, or they may not fruit. Always give new trees enough space for later growth. Small fruit is best treated as a unit and grown where it can later be caged in a wire netting enclosure to keep out birds, weeds inside the cage being suppressed by mulching. Loganberries and blackberries, however, are best grown outside, trained against fences or walls.

● **Simple vegetable growing.** Most gardening books give equal emphasis to every vegetable, failing to point out to the novice that there are degrees of difficulty in their cultivation. Some vegetables may be grown without being first raised in a heated greenhouse in special seed compost, and some may not; some are more or less immune from attack by particular pests and diseases, and others have to be nursed along and protected by spraying. The man with a new garden and without those aids to advanced gardening, the greenhouse and the cold frame, should know that by choosing the easiest vegetables to grow he can begin immediately to provide food for his family through the year; although if the ground is very rough he may have to be content the first year with a cleansing crop of potatoes only, which will prepare the soil for mixed crops the next year.

Table II gives a general idea of the degree of difficulty involved in growing some of the most common garden vegetables. However, it should be borne in mind, here and throughout, that there are broad regional variations in climate and soil. Before planning your garden, you should investigate growing conditions in your area. The Department of Agriculture maintains an agricultural extension service in each state which provides farm advisers (also called county or extension agents) who are available for consultation. Numerous publications can also be obtained from these services (see Appendix) or from the Superintendent of Documents, Government Printing Office (GPO), Washington, DC 20-402. Most are free or cost less than a dollar.

Table II   EASY AND DIFFICULT VEGETABLES

Group One: Very easy vegetables. These are relatively free from particular pests and diseases, are uncomplicated in cultivation, and need no glass or heat in their first stages.
Salads: Radish, all kinds of lettuce, spring onion.
Roots: Jerusalem artichoke, beet, parsnip, rutabaga, salsify, scorzonera, turnip.
Stems and bulbs: Garlic, rhubarb, shallot.
Legumes: Broad bean, snap bean. (Pick off tops of broad beans when plants have reached full growth to deter blackfly.)
Leaves: All kinds of cabbage and kale, broccoli, all herbs.

Group Two: Less easy vegetables.
Roots: Carrot (guard against fly), potato (spray against blight).
Stems and bulbs: Onion, kohlrabi.
Legumes: Pea, early and main-crop, scarlet runner (all need to be staked).
Leaves: Brussels sprout, spinach, cauliflower, chicory.
Various: Summer squashes, globe artichoke, pumpkin, strawberry, watercress, corn, tomato, eggplant, melon.

Group Three: More difficult vegetables. These need to be raised under glass in special compost, are selective in their soil needs or require special treatment in cultivation.
Celery, cucumber, asparagus, leek.

The gardener who for the first year or two grows only the vegetables in group one will be able to sow nearly all his seeds in the rows where the plants are to grow, though some cabbages will do well in a special seed bed of finely raked soil in the open, from which the seedlings will need to be transplanted.

(If, however, he particularly wants to raise one or two plants of group three he can do so by starting them in a box or tray of seed compost in any window of the house so long as the room has at least 6 hours of direct sunlight each day and is at a constant warm temperature. Place a layer of easily drained soil in the bottom of the tray and cover this with a ¾-in. layer of washed fine sand or shredded sphagnum moss, pressing it down to make a firm, smooth seedbed. Draw some ½-in. furrows in this, then water thoroughly and allow to drain. Sow seeds sparsely in the rows and cover lightly with more sand or moss. Sprinkle lightly with water and cover the tray with a sheet of clear plastic film, which will hold moisture in the soil and air around the seeds. Now place the covered tray in the window, where it will need no further attention until after the seedlings have grown their first true leaves. They can then be transplanted into pots and placed in a hotbed, a cold frame or under cloches until they are ready to be hardened off and planted in the open.)

● **Some gardening procedures.** Information as to plant varieties, sowing and planting out distances, special cultivation and season of growth, is to be found in any good gardening handbook or seed catalog. Every gardener should have a reliable handbook with plenty of line illustrations in the text. Among the many fine books now available are *The Organic Gardener* by Catherine Osgood Foster and *The New Vegetable & Fruit Garden Book* by R. Milton Carleton. Both these writers emphasize the need for the conservation of soil fertility and the production of healthy fruit and vegetables by the use of organic manures and home-made compost rather than chemical fertilizers. There is no doubt that organic gardening is not only biologically sounder than gardening with chemicals but is cheaper and more self-sufficient. The making of compost is a central activity in good gardening, for compost not only provides all the plant foods found in farmyard manure, it improves soil texture by encouraging the presence of earthworms, it holds moisture, and it conserves heat in the soil which is so important for early crops. Compost-grown vegetables are in general healthier and tastier, if not always larger, than vegetables grown without it. More, there is an inherent satisfaction in composting in that it turns materials which would otherwise be wasted to good account, feeding them back into the natural cycle of life.

● **Making compost.** Compost can be made in a brick, metal or wooden bin, or two or more bins placed side by side, each not less than 4 ft. sq., for smaller bins will not heat up or retain their heat so well.

The simplest bin is made by driving four metal stakes into the ground and fastening round these a length of 4-ft. fence netting to make a square basket which can then be lined with hardboard, plywood or tough cardboard. A more satisfactory bin is made with ½-in. boards sawed to length and nailed to four upright 3-by-3-in. corner posts on three sides. Leave the front open to receive slats cut to 1–2 in. less than 4 ft., and drop these in from the top between vertical runners as the heap is built up. The bin must be based on earth, and a horizontal air channel made at the base by parallel bricks placed on edge, the end bricks protruding beneath the bottom front slat. Brush some preservative other than creosote over the wood, and follow with a coat of paint to prevent rotting. When the box is ready, start the heap at the bottom with some coarse woody material and continue by throwing in any organic wastes that will decompose: lawn mowings, hedge clippings, clean and diseased vegetable leaves and stems, kitchen refuse, waste hay and straw, soaked newspapers, rotten fruit, etc. The dry compost should be wetted throughout until it holds no more moisture than a squeezed-out sponge.

With two boxes you can throw material at random into the first box, and when it is full, use it for building a heap more carefully in the second box. The vegetable material needs animal matter as an "activator" to start off and maintain the process of microbial fermentation which produces heat. All animal manures, including human, and particularly human urine—which should be diluted before sprinkling on—are activators and may be added in the proportion of 1 part animal to 4 parts vegetable matter. To build the heap methodically in the second box, then, begin with woody material, then add a 9-in. layer of vegetable matter from the top of the first box, scatter on this a thin layer of animal dung, follow with another thick layer of vegetation, sprinkle this with slaked lime and a spadeful of earth, add more vegetable matter, then more dung, and so on until the box or bin is full. Let the heap sink, and in a few days add more stuff in the same way.

Build the heap around a vertical air channel made with a length of piping which can afterwards be withdrawn. Be sure to keep the heap moist; cover with sacks or old matting to retain heat, and in wet weather fit a rough roof of corrugated iron or of planks covered with roofing felt. After about 6 months, when fermentation is over and the compost has cooled, it should contain worms which have crawled into it from the soil beneath. It can then be shoveled into a wheelbarrow from ground level if two or more of the top retaining slats are removed and the bottom ones pushed upwards and wedged in place.

● **Compost from hens.** Gardeners who keep a few hens in a wired run with access to pasture can produce compost by littering the run with straw, bracken and garden weeds and scattering the birds' grain on this. In scratching, the birds break up the litter which is then mixed by their feet with their droppings. If litter is constantly added, the surface of the run is kept fresh and clean, while as the litter deepens its lower layers are turned to compost on the spot. Clean out the run once a year, wet the material and stack it in a pile to generate heat and complete the composting. In this way each bird will produce ½ ton of compost a year.

● **Organic manures.** Strawy stable and farmyard manure, and horse manure that has been used for mushroom growing, should be brought in when possible. It should be mixed with compost, as should any goat and rabbit manure. Poultry droppings and pigeon dung are both useful activators for the compost heap but are too fierce to use directly on the soil without being stored first for a year in a dry bin. Wood ash should be kept dry until wanted for use on the onion bed, and soot, too, should be stored dry for a year before using.

Leaf mold makes a good peatlike mulch; small amounts may be put on the compost heap, but very large quantities of leaves should be tipped in the autumn into a wire cage where they will stay put and rot down for use as mulch next year. Seaweed is rich in minerals, but not in humus; it is a compost activator. Some of our coastal sea sands contain calcareous and animal matters which are of benefit to soils and plants. Marl, a species of muddy, clayey subsoil containing calcium carbonate and other elements, can be used for soil improvement, while some districts possess deposits of volcanic subsoil which can be dug up and spread on soils with good effect. Lawrence D. Hills advocates growing giant Russian comfrey for compost and for laying fresh in the trench where potatoes are to be grown. Commercial organic fertilizers which can be applied direct or used in compost heaps are: dried blood, hoof and horn meal, wool shoddy, bone meal and steamed bone flour, and fish manure. Green manuring is a quick method of making humus and supplying nitrogen to the soil by first sowing broadcast, and then shallowly digging in on the ground where it grows, a crop such as rape, mustard, lupin, buckwheat or winter vetches, or a mixture such as clover and rye grass; it is dug or disc-harrowed in while still lush, before flowering.

● **Minimum cultivation.** Nearly all old gardening

books begin with a chapter stressing the need for deep digging of gardens every year, but modern gardeners are beginning to discover that this is by no means necessary. It takes a man 30 days to double-dig an acre of heavy land, 18 days to dig it one spit deep. Why go to great lengths to aerate and break up the soil (and then compact it again with boots and rollers) when in an average healthy soil there are millions of workers, the worms, already doing it for you? Digging deeply and burying top growth to a depth where it cannot easily rot into humus, it is now widely believed, breaks up soil structure and interferes with the capillary action by which moisture at a depth can percolate upwards to nourish the roots of plants in a dry season. The school of "no-diggers" points out that unaided nature manages to produce forests of enormous trees without any form of soil cultivation; so why should man dig and plow in order to grow his corn and potatoes?

The answer seems to be that digging and plowing are initially necessary to make a clearing in wild nature and to suppress unwanted growths. It is easier to sow and cover seeds in a loose, friable soil than in a compact one. It is evident that every modern no-digger must have begun with a piece of land that at some time has been under cultivation. In practice the success of the method seems to depend on the large-scale manufacture of compost, of which there must be enough to make a permanent 1–2-in. layer over the whole garden. To manufac-

ture this may be as much work as digging the garden! As well as compost, then, mulches of leaf
mold, straw and even sawdust are used. Sawdust
takes nitrogen from the soil, and if used (with dis-
crimination) must be seasoned for a year by being
spread on paths before being thrown onto the garden. Where compost is short, Shewell-Cooper for
one recommends the use of sedge (not sphagnum)
peat, the seeds being sown on the soil surface and
then covered with a 1-in. layer of damp peat in
which a fish meal fertilizer has been mixed. Brassicas, etc., are dibbled into the peat in such a way
that their roots just penetrate the soil beneath.
Fresh supplies of peat are needed yearly to make
good the quantity converted into humus by worms.

● **How much to grow.** Having marked out the
plots for your four-course rotation and opted for
the easy vegetables in group one with one or two
from group two, a cropping plan is needed which
will ensure a year-round supply of vegetables, not
forgetting the hungry gap of late winter and early
spring. For a family of four or five persons the following table (Table III) may be taken as a guide.

In such a garden plan there will still be room for
successive sowings of lettuce, radish and spring
onion through the summer. (If the garden is too
small to grow all these crops, omit the eleven rows
of late potato and buy cheap potatoes for winter
use in bulk from a farmer.) Such a plan provides

Table III CROPPING PLAN FOR GARDEN OF ABOUT 500 SQ. YD.
PROVIDING VEGETABLES FOR A FAMILY OF 4–5 PERSONS

Vegetable	Quantity needed	No. of 30-ft. rows needed	Quantity of seed or no. of plants required
Jerusalem artichoke	112 lb	4	14 lb
Potato, early	336 lb	8	32 lb.
Potato, late	560 lb	11	33 lb
Cabbages of all kinds*	200 heads	10	200 plants
Kale	40 lb	2	40 plants
Kohlrabi	10 lb	1	⅛ oz
Leek	72 lb	4	240 plants
Onion	224 lb	6	6 lb sets or ¾ oz seed
Shallot	42 lb	2	4 lb bulbs
Rutabaga	112 lb	4	1 oz
Beet*	56 lb	2	1 oz
Parsnip	56 lb	2	½ oz
Carrot*	84 lb	4	1 oz
Broad bean*	120 lb	4	1 pint
Scarlet runner	140 lb	4	1 pint
Pea*	112 lb	4	2 pints

Successive sowings required

for summer vegetables from May onward, when kohlrabi and the first broad beans appear, an abundance of late summer and autumn produce, roots and potatoes for winter storage, with parsnips and artichokes still to be dug in the garden up to April, and with cabbages for cutting right through from June to the first frost.

● **Storing vegetables.** Vegetables that can be left to stand outside for winter use include parsnips (which can be dug and heaped in crisscross piles and left to get well frosted), Jerusalem artichokes and, south of New Jersey, kale and savoy cabbages. Vegetables that can be planted late and harvested on or after the first frost include brussels sprouts, escarole, late cabbages and Jerusalem artichokes. Other vegetables must be harvested before the frosts and those not needed until the spring (part of the potato crop, beets, carrots,) kept in an outdoor pit away from the house, while vegetables for winter use need to be near at hand in storeroom or cellar.

The temperature in a storeroom should be even, the atmosphere moist (especially for roots) and ventilation free. A dirt floor will keep air moist; with a cement floor, sand, soil or moss should be used in packing vegetables. Where no store cellar exists a small one can be dug outdoors in the side of a deep bank, or a 6 ft. 6 in. high cellar dug underground, lined with concrete blocks and roofed with a flat reinforced concrete slab. Walls and roof must be strong enough to hold the weight of earth shoveled back over the top. No windows are needed but there must be a normal door approached down a flight of concrete steps. Litter the floor with peat and over this place a false floor of wood slats. For ventilation, build an air vent into one wall leading into a pipe made to protrude through the ground, its top screened to keep out mice and birds.

● **Treatment of vegetables for storing.** Twist off the green tops of beets and turnips and pack sound roots in boxes with dry sand or wood ash to prevent shriveling or frost damage. Cut summer squashes before the first frost, leaving 2 in. of stem, and hang them in nets. Twist or plait the stems of onions round a central string, or pack into old nylon stockings and hang up on the wall. Stuff French and snap bean plants whole into a large sack until it is full; tie it at the neck and hang it from a nail while you beat it back and front with a stick until it is quite flat. Tip out the beans from the bottom of the sack, blow off the dust with bellows, and store the beans in large tins.

● **Storing roots outdoors.** Large quantities of potatoes or roots for stock feed may be stored outdoors in piles (clamps) covered with straw and earth. Lift the main-crop potatoes on a dry day when the haulms are ripe and the skins on the tubers are set. Select a patch of ground away from the drip of trees and not likely to be flooded in winter. Lay straw or ashes on the ground to a depth of 2 in. and arrange the tubers on this in a conical heap. Cover with a 6-in. thickness of straw and dig a drainage ditch near to it, covering the straw with earth taken from the ditch. Leave a tuft of straw to stick up through a vent hole at the top, but seal this with earth before heavy frosts come. Mangels, fodder beet, etc., are stored in the same way.

● **To store cabbages outdoors,** pull them out root and all and set them side by side with their roots in a shallow trench, packing loose soil around the roots. Then build a rough frame about 2 ft. high around the trench with boards or poles, and bank this with soil. Place poles across the top of the frame to hold a covering of straw or bracken.

● **Storing fruit.** Late varieties of pears and apples will usually store well, but allow the picked fruits to cool and sweat overnight before stowing them away in a cool, dark, well-aired place protected from mice and rats. Store fruit separately from vegetables. If stored in boxes, wrap each fruit individually in newspaper; if on shelves, do not allow fruits to touch one another. Avoid upstairs rooms or dry places which will shrivel the fruit. Inspect once a week and remove all rotten fruits.

● **Saving seed.** In normal times it is better to buy seed than to save your own, but it sometimes happens that scarlet runner seed, for example, is in short supply, and those who have wisely let some of their bean pods dry out on the haulm for the sake of their ripe seeds will not be affected by the general scarcity. With potatoes it is thrifty to save each autumn most of your seed needs for the following year from the most productive plants in the garden, buying the other half, as good seed potatoes are increasingly hard to come by. Again, with packet seeds it is advisable to buy new seeds each spring, for the life-span of seeds varies, and unless you are certain of the age of seeds and know their life-span (1 year for parsnips to 7 years for summer squashes), it may prove a waste of time to sow them. If, however, you do decide one year to save some of your own seeds, remember to distinguish between self-pollinating vegetables which reproduce themselves almost exactly through their seeds, and those which cross-pollinate and cannot be relied upon to breed true to type unless they are carefully isolated during growth. Peas, beans, tomatoes, lettuce are normally self-pollinated; cabbage, broccoli, turnips, cucumbers, onions, parsnips, beets, summer squashes are cross-pollinators. If seed is to be saved from one or two selected plants in the second group, they should be protected from unwanted cross-pollination by tying the flower heads in a muslin or polythene bag. Plants that have been let run to seed are hung head downwards in a dry shed with newspaper spread on the floor to catch the seeds as the plant dries out and they fall. Store them in lidded jars or tins.

Part IV:

BREAD, BEER AND TOBACCO

□12□

FROM SEED TO BREAD LOAF

The farm laborer of 60 years ago who had a half acre or more of garden or allotment with a pigsty at one end would sometimes divide the area into two and grow wheat and vegetables alternately on each part, having prepared the ground by spreading the pig manure and digging it in in the autumn. He would sow the wheat broadcast or use a 3-ft. dibble in each hand and a fixed central line, walking backwards around and about the line in a widening "square circle"—the pattern of plowing—followed by a helper to drop the seeds into the dibble holes; or he would use a hand drill. He would harvest the ripe crop with a sickle or a reaping hook and beat out the wheat from the husk with a flail—implements which had been superseded on the farm but which survived in the farmworker's yard.*

* See George Ewart Evans, *The Farm and the Village* (London: Faber, 1969).

From his quarter acre he would get a yield of perhaps 10 bushels of wheat, which he would get the miller to grind into household flour for bread and puddings, the coarse offal being fed to the pig.

Anyone who has a half-acre garden can still do the same, except that he will now have to grind his flour at home. The seed needed would be 2½ pecks. Since it takes a pound of flour to make a 1¼-lb. loaf and 10 bushels of wheat = 600 lb., allowing for wastage there would still be enough flour to make at least 1½ loaves daily throughout the year. And the very best sort of loaves, longer keeping, tastier and more nourishing than any bought bread.

Nor need one grow wheat only. Rye and barley make good bread, and may be used whole or mixed with wheat flour. Corn also may be grown, ground into flour, and mixed with wheat flour to make bread.

● **Growing wheat.** Wheat is simple to grow but it needs heavy soil or good loam. Barley requires a light loam, while rye will grow on lighter soil. Different varieties of wheat suit different localities and soil types—so consult a local expert or obtain seed from a neighboring farmer who knows his oats.

Spring wheat needs sowing as soon as the ground can be properly worked, after which time it is better to sow barley. Deep cultivation of the soil is not necessary; as with other crops, there should be plenty of moisture-holding organic matter in the soil surface.

Sow with a hand drill set for 4 in. between rows, taking a line in the center of the plot and following in a "square circle" round and round it to save pauses at the end of each row. Rake the plot, and roll it if you like. Take steps to scare away birds while the wheat is growing. Deal with large weeds like thistles and docks in June/July; smaller weeds will be suppressed by the wheat.

Cut the wheat as soon as the grain is hard enough to rub out of the ear when rolled between the hands. The traditional harvesting tool is not the scythe but the serrated-edged sickle (Fig. 11). Such sickles are still made by T. & J. Hutton & Co. Ltd, Ridgeway, Sheffield, England among others. A practiced scythesman can work, it is true, about twice as fast as a man or woman with a sickle, cut-

Fig. 11

ting two acres to the sickle user's one. Barley and
rye are more quickly cut than wheat. With a two-
handed scythe you cut the stalks close to the
ground, letting them fall in a long swath. With the
one-handed sickle the action is different. Bending
over, you grasp a bunch of ears with one hand,
thrust in the sickle with the other and draw it towards you with a gentle sawing motion, severing
the stalks with the least spillage of grain. It is usual
to cut near ground level, to bind the stalks and ears
into sheaves and lean them together in shocks; but
with a sickle you can cut as high as you please,
merely taking off the ears if you prefer. But as
wheat straw is valuable it is best to follow normal
practice and thresh out the grain from the full
stems, which can be afterwards stacked and used.
Unlike the scythe or the smooth reaping hook, the
sickle needs no sharpening during the period of
use.

Harvesting goes well if two people work together, one cutting the stalks, the other gathering
and tying the sheaves. A sheaf is a full double arm-
ful of stems clasped to the body and tied by touch
at the far side with straw rope or binder twine. If
full of weeds, tie sheaves smaller and leave to stand
until the weeds have withered. Do not stack the
sheaves until grain is hard with the straw all dead.
Wet or weedy sheaves may generate heat when
stacked, and spoil. Stacking is best done under an
open-sided shed with a hard floor, or in the open

on a square of polythene and with a black
polythene or tarpaulin cover. The object of stacking
is to store the wheat until such time as the grain
can be threshed out from the straw, and the sooner
this is done the better.

To thresh, untie the sheaves singly or in pairs,
and spread them indoors on a clean flat floor or
outdoors on a canvas tilt. Whack out the grain from
the ears either with a single stick, or with a double,
jointed stick called a flail (Fig. 12), which can be
made by taking a stout ash stick (the handle) and
an equally stout stick of tough holly or hawthorn
half its length (the "swingle" or "swiple"), and
jointing them with a piece of pigskin or eelskin or

Fig. 12

other tough flexible material in such a way that it forms a universal joint, allowing movement of the swingle in any direction. The flail needs practice in its use, but when mastered does its work well. Having knocked out all the grain from the sheaves against the threshing floor, stack the straw and winnow the grain—i.e., free it from husks, bits of straw, weed seeds and dust—by tossing it in a draft which is just strong enough to blow away the trash without disturbing the grain. Where there is current, an electric fan or vacuum cleaner can be brought into service. The winnowed grain must then be stored in lidded bins until wanted for grinding. The labor of flailing can be saved by investing in a miniature grain thresher which can be clamped onto a workbench and worked by hand or a small electric engine.

● **Grinding grain.** When there is nothing else to use one can grind grain in a fixed, hollow stone or "saddle" using a flat moving stone or "muller," the most primitive of all grinding devices. The quern, first used about 2,000 years ago, was the first hand mill proper, consisting of two flat circular stones, the lower of which was slightly dished while the upper one was pierced in the center and turned on a wood or metal pin. The operator dropped grain with one hand into the hole and with the other revolved the upper stone by means of a stick pushed into a small hole near the edge. Such stones, if found on ancient sites and fitted together, can still be used. It is no longer possible to go to a hardware store and buy a simple hand mill; but a small one, the Corona hand mill, is available from Smithfield Implement Co., 99 N. Mark St., Smithfield, UT 84-335. For kitchen use, a coffee mill or a mincer fitted with a grain-grinding plate will grind small quantities. Some electric mixers have an attachment which will grind wheat, and Lee Engineering Co., 2023 W. Wisconsin Ave., Milwaukee, WI 53201, makes several models of electric flour mills producing either 3–5 or 6–10 lb. per hour. The flour ground will be whole wheat including the bran; a finer flour is obtained by sieving.

BAKING

● **Whole wheat bread.** To make standard whole wheat loaves, take 3 lb. flour, 1 tbsp. molasses or 1 level tbsp. soft brown sugar, 1 level tbsp. salt, 1 oz. fat (lard, margarine or butter), 2 pints lukewarm water, 2 oz. fresh baker's yeast or 1 oz. dried yeast. Warm a large mixing bowl or pot. Then:

1. Put flour in bowl and stand it in a warm place.

2. Blend the yeast with 1 tsp. of the sugar or molasses and dissolve in ⅓ pint of warm water. Mix well and stand in a warm place until the yeast

is working—about 5–10 minutes. Do not allow to get hot or the yeast will be killed.

3. Rub the fat into the warmed flour.

4. Dissolve salt and sugar or molasses in the remaining warm water.

5. Make a well in the flour and pour in the salted water together with the yeast water.

6. Mix with wooden spoon, then knead well in the bowl. There is no need to turn out onto a floured board to knead the dough. If the dough sticks to the side of the bowl, simply lift it away from the bottom and sprinkle a handful of extra flour into the bowl as often as required. Knead only for a few minutes until the dough is smooth and neither too wet nor too dry. Cover bottom of bowl with another thin layer of flour, on which the dough should rest; then leave the bowl covered with a damp cloth in a warm place until the dough has risen to twice its size or more.

7. Meanwhile, grease and warm three 2-lb. bread pans.

8. When the dough has risen, knead lightly again, then divide into thirds and place in the pans. The dough in each pan should come a little less than halfway up the sides. If preferred, two 2-lb. tins and one 1-lb. tin can be used, the remaining dough being made into ten or twelve rolls each the size of a small apple.

9. Set the pans once more in a warm place until the dough has barely risen to the top of the pans

and the rolls, if any, are twice their original size.

10. Bake in a hot oven preheated to about 375° F for 30–35 minutes for loaves, 25–30 minutes for rolls.

11. Turn out on a wire rack to cool.

● **Types of oven.** The quantities given in the above recipe are suitable for the cook with a stove which is kept burning all the time. Our forebears who baked only once a week or even less frequently, and made large quantities of bread at a time, did so to economize on fuel. The brick bread oven still remaining in some old cottages is a long tunnel, without grating or chimney, built into the wall, and is preheated by a fierce fire of twigs. Having lit the twigs, you close the door; when the fire is burnt out, take off the door and either rake out the ashes or brush them to one side before putting in the shaped dough and any other food which is to be cooked. Cooking is done wholly by the heat retained in the bricks. A "tin" loaf is of course one baked in a tin, and a "cottage" loaf one baked on the stone floor of the oven.

Before the coming of the iron range in the late nineteenth century, cottages without brick ovens were supplied with a clay baking oven which retained heat in the same way as bricks after sticks had been burned in it. Its attainment of sufficient heat for baking is tested by scraping the top with a dry stick; if the stick sparks, it is time to take out the embers, wipe the oven out with a damp mop, push in the loaves, reposition the door and plaster it in place with clay. Such ovens are now rare.

If you have no oven but only an open hearth with cooking pots, then dough in tins can be baked in a big flat-topped fish kettle over which hot embers can be piled. Time of baking varies with the heat of the oven and the size of the loaves, but the oven should be hot (400° F) for the first 10 minutes, preferably getting less hot, like the brick oven, as baking continues. At 375–400° F, a 1¼–lb loaf will bake in 45–60 minutes. Fresh yeast will rise quicker than old. Do not let the dough rise too much, put it in the oven when it has doubled its size. A loaf is done if it sounds hollow when tapped.

● **Potato bread** (a Victorian recipe). Get 3/5 pint of yeast fresh from the brewhouse, weighing not less than 3½ oz. Boil 1 lb. potatoes in their skins. Place potatoes in a wood pail, add ½ lb. flour and pound them with the end of a rolling pin. Add 2½ quarts cold water and mix well. Put 1 peck flour into a pan, make a hole in the middle place two sticks across the top, set a sieve over them and strain the liquor into the hole. Now add the ½ pint yeast and stir in enough flour to make a thin batter. Cover, and leave for 2 hours to ferment. Add 1½ oz. salt and enough water to make the flour into dough. Knead. Cover with a cloth and let rise for 1½ hours. Knead again and throw out onto the board, divide into loaves, let rise, and bake in a moderate oven from 20–40 minutes.

Bread without kneading. For each 1 lb. flour use 1 pint warm water, ½ oz. yeast, ¼ oz salt. Mix yeast with a cup of the warm water and allow to work. Mix dry flour and salt in a bowl, make a hole in the middle, pour the yeast into it and stir in from the sides to make a smooth paste. Slowly add the rest of the water and mix into a smooth wet dough, and let it rise in the bowl, covered with a damp cloth, until it doubles in size (20 minutes). Having ready some greased tins, spoon the dough into them and allow 10–15 minutes to settle. Bake for 40–50 minutes.

Baking powder bread. For every 1 lb. flour, use 2 tsp. baking powder, 1 tsp. salt and about 3/5 pint milk. Well mix the flour, salt and baking powder. Moisten with milk to a stiffish dough, knead rapidly and divide into loaves. Place in greased tins and bake at 425° F for 1 hour.

Corn flour and wheat bread. Pour 5 quarts boiling water on 7 lb. corn flour, stirring all the time. Let it stand until lukewarm, then mix into it 14 lb. fine wheat flour previously mixed with ¼ lb. salt. Hollow the surface of the mixture and pour into it 2½ quarts yeast thickened to a cream with flour. Let it stand overnight. Next morning knead the mass and let stand for 3 hours. Divide into loaves and let them stand in tins for ½ hour, then bake as with other breads.

Breakfast cereals. Almost any whole grain can be turned into a ready-to-serve breakfast cereal by simply exploding it in an iron or steel saucepan set over low heat for a few minutes with the lid on. Add a trace of salad oil and shake the pan now and then to prevent sticking. **Porridge:** Boil a little more than 1 pint water in a thick pan, add 1 level tsp. salt (or mix salt beforehand with dry oatmeal), slowly sprinkle in 2 oz. *medium* oatmeal, stirring continuously. When boiling again, reduce heat, put lid on pan and allow to simmer for 1 hour, stirring frequently (at least every 10 minutes). Rather than a spoon use a 12-in. length of smooth ¾-in. doweling with the end rounded, on which the cooking oatmeal cannot clog. **Muesli:** With a small nut mill you can grind wheat, flax and sunflower seeds; add some milled nuts, dried or fresh fruit, and let the lot soak in milk.

Frumenty: Put some ripe wheat into an earthenware jar, top with water, and let stand in an oven or on a stove overnight or until the grains burst. Eat hot or cold with milk and sugar.

□13□

GROWING & CURING TOBACCO

The habit of smoking is one which it is better not to acquire, as it is injurious both to health and to the pocket. If acquired, the habit should be broken from time to time, for the state of dependence on a weed is not one which a moral being should permit in himself. One way of appeasing a craving for tobacco is to smoke a herbal mixture mainly consisting of dried coltsfoot, which grows along many country lanes. Commercial herbal tobaccos almost all contain these ingredients: 3½ oz. coltsfoot mixed with ½ oz. each of eyebright, buckbean, betony (germander), rosemary, wild thyme, lavender and camomile flowers. Using this recipe as a standard you can make up your own mixture to taste. While pleasant enough to smoke, the chief use of herbal tobaccos is as a remedy for asthma and other breathing troubles—to which end they need not be smoked at all but shaken loosely into a saucer and burned near the sufferer. Another tobacco substitute is the silks of sweet corn.

● **Cultivation.** It is legal to grow tobacco for your own use, but the production and sale of tobacco products is federally regulated. Tobacco seeds are minute, ½ oz. of them providing plants for an acre of ground, so you will need only a pinch of seed. The seeds are first mixed with fine sand and sown in fine compost in a heated greenhouse or under cloches, being later transplanted to the field. Seedlings reach transplant size 8–10 weeks after planting. Find out when transplanting is best begun in your area (anywhere from late March in the southernmost regions to June in northern locations) so you will know when to start your seeds. As they grow, harden them off in preparation for planting. Tobacco can be grown in most soils but needs plenty of potash. Set the plants out in double rows 2 ft. apart, staggering them 18 in. apart in the rows. Leave 4 ft. between each double row. The plant should grow straight up in a single stalk ending in a flower head, so pick off any side branches. Full growth of 5 ft. or more is reached about 2 months after transplanting. At this point, nip off the flower head. The lower leaves will then begin to ripen and change color. Before the leaf turns yellow, break it off close to the stem. Remove the leaves higher on the stem as they too ripen.

Drying or curing. When picked, thread the leaves in pairs back to back, with about a dozen leaves to each foot of string, and hang them up in a dark, airy shed for 6–8 weeks to dry. Take care that not only leaves but stalks are quite free of moisture— they should be stiff and leathery.

Dry leaves are brittle and break when handled. Remoisten them by putting them in an open shed overnight to absorb moisture from the air, or lay them on the floor and cover with a damp sheet for 3 or 4 hours, after which they should be fit for handling. Now make them into "hands" by tying together the butt ends of thirty or forty leaves.

Fermentation and maturing. The cured tobacco can now be used, but it gives a rough smoke. Though its quality can be much improved if it is further fermented in a kiln, this cannot well be done at home. Unfermented tobacco may be crudely prepared for smoking by taking down the dried hands when required and stirring and squeezing them in a bucket of cold water until they take on the appearance of chamois leather, then wringing out the moisture and slicing the leaves finely on a board with a blade taken from a jack plane. The fine-cut tobacco so produced can be teased out and dried in the sun within minutes, ready for smoking, or allowed to dry slowly at room temperature.

□14□

BEER & WINE

Alcohol is both a stimulant and a preservative, and all wines, beers and ciders are to some extent foods as well as digestive aids.

Both beer and wine have a venerable history in the United States. There is no evidence that American Indians brewed beer, but the Pilgrims brought it with them on the *Mayflower*, and it has been here since. Later European immigrants brought with them vines of the Old World species and centuries of experience to add to the native art of wine making. Today the United States produces more beer than any other country, ranks eleventh in per capita consumption, and in the production and consumption of wine places sixth and thirty-first, respectively. The home brewing of beer is generally illegal, but federal law permits the head of a household to make up to 200 gal. of wine per year.

126

A. BREWING BEER

Beer is the fermented product of the three chief ingredients: barley, hops and water. It is possible, given the land, to grow and harvest a patch of barley and a row of hops, to malt the barley and to brew in a day enough beer of the best quality for a year's supply: this is best done in autumn. Or one could buy the barley and hops and malt the barley oneself; or, at greater cost, buy the prepared malt. But the costliest method of home brewing is still far cheaper than buying the finished product, and the taste of the beer will be incomparably better.

To grow barley. Suppose you work out your annual household need for beer as 79 gal. (= 1 1/5 quart per day). This figure may be reduced proportionately as you please. Now, it takes roughly 4 bushels of malt and 4 lb. of hops to brew 60–72 gal. of ale in two workings, and 4 bushels of barley produces rather more than that quantity, by measure, of dry malt. To grow 4–5 bushels of barley you will need about 1/12 acre of good land; and on this you may grow also a single row of hops: which, however, will not give a crop until the third year. Of barley seed you will need about 1½ pecks (= about 20 lb.).

Barley needs a moderately dry and warm climate, and a light loamy soil with some lime. In the old four-course rotation it followed the turnip crop. Two-rowed types such as Erie are favored malting varieties. Broadcast or drill the seed in early spring; all being well it will germinate and be showing green within three or four days. If the ground is clean to start with the growth of the barley will stifle weeds and will need little attention until harvest. Allow the barley to stand until the grain is fully ripe, and cut with a scythe. Leave it in the swath for a few days, then carry it off and store it in a shed until you are ready to thresh out the grain. Tie the stalks tightly together in bundles, hang the barley up with the ears dangling and thresh onto an outspread sheet with a stick or improvised jointed flail, damaging the grain as little as possible. Store grain in a ratproof container.

To grow hops. If dried hops are easy to obtain, buy them. If not, a row can be grown on wires strained between two 8-ft. end posts. Hops need a deep, rich, heavily manured soil with good drainage, preferably in a south or southwest facing position with some shelter and a free circulation of air. Plants are obtained from cuttings or suckers taken from healthy old stools (for hops are perennials), and as they make little growth in the first year, may be planted closely together in a nursing line for twelve months before planting out where they are to flower.

Your row, with a reinforced post at each end, should have staunch poles at intervals to take the weight of the full-grown bine. Stretch a wire from post to post at a height of 6 in. from the ground, a second wire 6 ft. from the ground and a third along the tops of the posts. Plant out suckers in groups of from three to five, a few inches apart, at intervals of 6 ft. Female plants are needed as it is they which produce the cones, but a male or two should be included in the row. Tie a line of string vertically to the wires to provide leaders for the tendrils of the growing plants. Mulch the row and lightly fork the ground between the stools.

The cones are fit to pick when they are firm in substance and beginning to change in color from green to light amber. Only the cones are picked, leaves and lower branches being left on the stem, which is left standing so that the nutrients it contains may find a way back into the soil.

Hops must be dried at once or they will heat and quickly spoil, especially if picked when moist. Dry by spreading the crop out on wire netting frames and letting the heat from a charcoal brazier or paraffin stove rise through them, preferably where there is a draft to distribute the heat evenly. If overheated they will lose their essential bitter oil. Dry them overnight, allow to cool (the ends of the stalks must have become shriveled), then pack them tightly under pressure in netting sacks. Store in a dry place.

To malt barley. Soak the barley about 3 days, changing the water daily to keep the grain sweet;

then "couch" the barley—spread it out from 12–18 in. deep for 24–36 hours to generate the heat necessary for growth. The root will begin to grow from each grain, at which point the temperature must be lowered by "flooring," or spreading the grain thinly over the stone or brick floor, where it must be stirred and turned two or three times a day, the temperature being kept constant at 60° F meanwhile, to inhibit the growth of shoots. In 10 or 12 days the grain will have lost its moisture, when it should be heaped more thickly to generate heat until the embryonic shoot inside (which may be seen if a grain is held up to the light) is about three-quarters the size of the grain. Now oven-dry the grains for 3 or 4 days at not more than 180° F, with warm air passing through the grains. For this they are best spread out on shelves of fine wire grid, either in an oven with an open door, or on tiers over the source of heat. The finished malt must be crisp but unburnt. The darker the malt the darker the ale that will result, so if a pale ale is wanted, the malt needs to be roasted only to a pale amber color. After this drying the malt is screened from the rootlets and ground for use like coffee.

● **Equipment for brewing.** The essential process in brewing is the boiling of the malt in water to make the "wort," the infusion of hops in the wort, and its fermentation by the addition of yeast. How

much ale can be brewed at one time depends on
the size of one's boiler, to which the other utensils
will conform. In the absence of the old-fashioned
boiler holding up to 48 gal. one could use an ex-
army field kitchen of the type employed by farmers
for boiling up pig mash, or a metal tank raised on
bricks with a fire beneath it. If power is available,
an electric boiler is the thing. Lacking these, the last
resort is to brew a few gallons at a time in the
largest suitable vessel over the kitchen stove. Besides the boiler, one needs a mashing tub in which
to perform the first operation of steeping the malt
to make the wort which is afterwards boiled, a tun
into which the hop-infused ale is put to "work", or
ferment, and a shallow tub for a cooler, to allow the
heated wort to cool down to the right temperature
for the addition of yeast. Then you must have
enough casks of the right capacity to store the
liquor.

Oak casts need to be fumigated with sulphur,
sterilized with steam or boiling water, and then
swilled around with a little of the liquor they are to
contain. Barrels of inert plastic with alkathene caps
and spigots are suitable as casks; a tank made of
some good-quality hard plastic material will serve
for mashing ale, while large plastic trash cans with
lids are also useful in home brewing.

Brewing. If you plan to make 32 gal. at a
brew—to include a first brewing of ale proper and a

second brewing of "small beer" from the same malt—your boiler will need to be of 24 gal. capacity, your mashing tub of 36 gal., your tun of 18 gal., and your coolers of proportionate size. A bushel of malt is needed for such a brewing, and ¾ lb. hops. First fill the boiler with clear, preferably soft water and bring to a boil. Then put into the mashing tub one pail of the boiling water and enough cold water to reduce the temperature to 170° F. Tip in the bushel of malt and stir it well with a wooden stick. Leave for 15 minutes. Fill up the boiler again and bring it back to a boil. The 15 minutes having elapsed, add to the mashing tub enough boiling water to make your 11 gal. of first quality ale, allowing for the soaking up of 6 gal. by the grain: say 18 gal. Stir the malt again well. Cover the mashing tub with clean sacks and let it stand for 2 hours. Then siphon off the wort into buckets and pour it into the tun, where it will remain until the boiler is empty to receive it.

Now empty the water from the boiler into the mashing tub to make the second brewing, of small beer. (That is, if you can bear to drink small beer, which is really meant as a thirst-quencher for the sweating laborer in the field.)

The boiler being empty, put the ale wort from the first brewing into it, together with ¾ lb. of hops well rubbed and separated. Then bring the uncovered boiler to a brisk boil for 1 hour or more. Put out the fire, or switch off the current, and strain the liquor into the coolers through a wire or willow basket which will retain the hops.

When this liquor has cooled to 70° F, pour it into the tun. Add to this half a pint of working yeast (i.e., 2 oz. of yeast that has previously been mixed with a half pint of the warm wort so that it is now active) and stir the liquor to mix the yeast well in. Cover the top of the tub. In 6–8 hours a frothy head will rise, and will keep rising for 48 hours. After 24 hours, skim off the froth and put it into a pan; repeat in 12 hours, and then again, until the working has subsided. When the beer is cold it must be casked. The cask will be in your cellar or outhouse on its side, bunghole uppermost, placed on a stout square frame with foot-long legs and with wedges positioned on each side of the cask to stop it rolling. The bunghole must be slightly to one side so that excess liquid spills out in one direction, where it can be caught in a pail. Bring the beer down in buckets and pour it in through a funnel until the cask is full. The beer will resume working, and a gallon or two should be kept in hand to top up the cask. When working ceases, right the cask, bunghole uppermost, and wedge it in place. Thrust in a handful of fresh hops. Fill the cask quite full. Put in the bung, wrapped in cloth, and hammer it home.

Meantime the small beer is made by pouring 22 gal. of boiling water from the boiler onto the already used malt in the mashing tub. Stir the grains well, cover the tub and allow it to stand for 1 hour. Siphon or draw off the liquor and put it into the tun, as before. The boiler now again being empty, the first ale liquor having been taken out of it to cool, tip the small beer wort into it, with the used hops and a ¼ lb. of fresh hops, and boil briskly for an hour. Clean out the mashing tub and strain the liquor from the boiler into it. Throw away the strained-out hops and leave the small beer liquor to cool to 70° F, then pour in the working yeast as with the ale. Proceed as with the ale, but cask it while still just warm or it will not work in the barrel.

Substitutes for hops. Ale may be brewed without hops, as it was before the seventeenth century; but such ale, without the tonic, narcotic and astringent properties imparted by hops, will taste insipid. Lacking cultivated hops, wild hops may be used, or the ale may be made bitter by the use of tansy, wormwood, yarrow, marjoram or buckbean. Other plants which have been used to embitter ale are sweet gale and bracken root.

To make yeast. Brewer's yeast, or dried yeast sold for home brewing, is best, but baker's yeast can be used. Yeast can be made at home by boiling 1 oz. hops in 2½ quarts water for half an hour. Strain and let the liquor cool to body temperature. Add 1 tsp. salt and ¼ lb. sugar. Beat up ½ lb. plain flour with some of the liquor and then mix the lot all together in a bowl. After 48 hours, add 1½ lb. boiled mashed potatoes. Leave for 24 hours, strain and bottle it, corking tightly, so that it is ready for use when wanted. The liquor must be kept near a fire while it is making, and stirred frequently. Shake before using. The yeast will keep for 8 weeks in a cool place.

Bachelor brewing. As little as 4–5 gal. ale may be brewed at a time by using an aluminum pan on a stove, a plastic trash can, some polythene tubing and a dozen screw-top beer or cider bottles, with extract of malt either dry or bottled, and dried hops.

Pale ale. 2 lb. dried light malt extract, 3½ oz. hops, 2 lb. sugar, 1 pint tea, salt, yeast and water. Put hops in a muslin bag and boil for 15 minutes in just over 1 quart water. Put the hop water into the plastic trash can with the fresh tea. Add malt, sugar, a little salt and make up to 2½ gal. with boiling water. Stir, let cool to 70° F, and add yeast. Replace lid and allow liquor to ferment in a warm place for about 7 days. When fermenting ceases, syphon ale into screw-top bottles containing a little sugar, to make a head when poured.

Brown ale. 2 lb. dried dark malt extract, 1½ lb. brown sugar, 2 oz. hops, 1 tbsp. molasses, salt, yeast, water. Proceed as for pale ale, adding molasses at the same time as the malt.

B. MAKING CIDER

Cider (or apple wine) is the drink of the apple- or pear-growing regions as beer is of the grain-growing areas. The bitter apples grown for cider are unfit for eating raw or cooked, as are cider pears. Any apples will make cider so long as they are not too sweet, in which case a proportion of crab apples may be mixed in. Late apples are better than early ones.

Gather the apples and leave for a few days to mellow, then throw out any unsound ones.

Utensils and pressing. As fruit, unlike grain, is acid, care must be taken in the selection of utensils. Wooden casks and tubs are best, but enamel, stainless steel, silver- and tin-plate and aluminium utensils are acceptable, as are glass, earthenware and good-quality plastic. To crush the apples into pulp and to press out the juice a mill of some sort and a press are required. Lacking the first, you can pound one layer of apples at a time in a stout wooden tub with a balk of timber, but a more effective crusher may be made from an old mangle with a crude box hopper superimposed, and with chromium wood-screws let into the wooden rollers in a spiral pattern with heads projecting: when the handle is turned the apples, falling from the hopper, are caught up and shredded.

The resultant "pomace" is dumped in an open tub or tank with or without a little water, and left for a day and night so that fermentation may begin and further break down the fruit cells.

Next, the pomace is shoveled into coarse canvas or burlap bags, which are suspended over an empty tub to drain. This drained juice is put aside for the best quality cider. The bags are then squeezed in a press to extract the rest of the juice. The more pressure the more cider, but the coarser the quality due to seeds and skins.

Pressing may be done in a handscrew-operated cider press. A substitute for this can be made from two squares of thick, heavy hardwood between which the bag is pressed. One piece forms the baseplate, the other the pressure plate, and this has squared inlets cut out from two sides to allow it to slide freely up and down two strong squared wooden uprights between which it is captive, the bottoms of these uprights being fixed to the base while the tops are joined together by a crossbar. These uprights are reinforced at the top and bottom by iron angle brackets screwed to the outside of the frame, the bottom ones holding the frame to the base. This strengthening is essential. Grooves in the surface of the baseplate channel the juice to a point of outlet. The uprights must be high enough to allow a fair-sized bag of pulp to be placed between the two platforms, and also to permit the entry of the business end of a car jack in the space between the top platform and the strengthened crossbar. As the jack is wound up, so compression increases between crossbar and top plate, forcing the plate down on to the baseplate and so squashing the juice out from the bag of pulp.

Fermentation. The collected juice is now poured into casks and allowed to ferment spontaneously; large bungholes will allow the cider to froth over, as it will and must do, to be caught in vessels placed beneath. To help this, the casks must be topped up continually. The longer the cider is allowed to ferment the greater its alcoholic content will be. After somewhere between 3 and 10 days it is racked off from its sediment into clean casks and stored in a cool place. Bung tightly when all fermentation has ceased. In the following spring this cider is again racked, after which it is ready for drinking. Fermentation temperature is about 50° F. Rough cider is that in which too much acetic acid has been formed through fermentation at too high a temperature. Sweet cider results when only some of the natural sugar has been converted into alcohol, suggesting too low a fermenting temperature. Champagne cider is a good mellow cider bottled (in champagne bottles) before fermentation is complete.

Cider in small quantities. To make a gallon or two of cider, treat it as apple wine, using a wine yeast and other additives as directed for fruit wines (see next section). The washed, unpeeled apples may be pushed through a mincer or pulped in an electric juice extractor. If boiled water is added to the juice, some sugar and chopped sultanas will be needed. Apple wine may be altered in character by the addition of 1 lb. red fruit to every 4 lb. apples.

C. WINE

While the grape may seem to be the first choice of fruits for making wine, since it contains in its pips, skin and juice all the necessary ingredients for that purpose, I would advise those who wish simply to make a regular quantity of good, dry red wine for the table to concentrate upon wines made from blackberries, damsons or sloes, and elderberries, most of which can be obtained in quantity at little or no cost every autumn.

Blackberries are an easy crop to grow, either the cultivated varieties or wild brambles dug up and replanted in deep garden soil. Brambles are best grown on wires along a wall, but they make good hedges anywhere if grown along wires strained between posts. They need to be mulched, fed with liquid manure, and pruned: the old wood is cut right out after fruiting in autumn, next year's fruits being on the new shoots which must be trained along the wires to replace the old. Increase is by layering or dividing.

Country wines may, indeed, be made from many other fruits, vegetables and even flowers: with nearly all of them water is needed to increase the volume of juice and/or reduce its acidity, together with white cane or beet sugar to supplement any natural sugars which, in the fermentation process, are turned by yeasts into alcohol and waste carbon dioxide gas.

● **Equipment for making wines.** As with cider, wines must not come into contact with iron or copper utensils, and the same materials as for cider making should be used.

Apart from articles found in every kitchen, the wine maker or vintager needs:

1. A large crock or jug, or plastic bin, for the first fermentation.

2. Some cheesecloth or other close-woven material for straining and for squeezing out juice from crushed pulp.

3. One or more jars or casks for the main fermentation and for storing wine.

4. One or more special glass or plastic air locks with an equal number of holed corks for plugging the necks of those jars. (These air locks, when partly filled with water and pushed into the holed cork in the jars, permit gas to escape from the fermenting liquor while preventing airborne organisms from entering and infecting it.)

5. A 4-ft. length of ¼-in. clear polythene tubing for siphoning the wine off the sediment, or "lees," from one container to another.

6. A glass or plastic funnel.

7. A supply of wine bottles, with new straight-sided corks.

The making of wine is simplicity itself. The picked fruit is washed and all unripe and imperfect fruit rejected. It is then crushed and soaked in warm water so that the natural enzymes in the fruit are enabled to attack and break down the juice-retaining pectin in the tissues. This watery pulp is then pressed through muslin into a clean crock or bin where the generally cloudy liquid is now known as "must." To this must are added the required quantities of water and sugar: as a rough guide, a total amount of slightly over 1 gal. water and 2–3 lb. sugar to each 5–6 lb. of red fruit, if an efficient yeast is used. Into the must, kept at a room temperature of 65–75° F, some previously prepared active yeast is stirred—it may be baker's, brewer's, or preferably a special wine yeast. The crock or bin is covered with some thick cloth to protect the must while it undergoes its first, turbulent fermentation. Any froth is skimmed off. When fermentation steadies, the liquid is "racked," or siphoned off into one or more large fermentation jars, the necks of which are then either plugged with cotton wool, covered with polythene film held in place by a rubber band, or preferably corked and fitted with fermentation locks. Still at room temperature, the sweetened working must be allowed to "ferment out," that is, to work until the last of the sugar it contains has been converted to alcohol and carbon dioxide and no more bubbles rise in the jar. The wine is then racked from its lees into a clean empty jar, sealed and stored in a cool place and left for some months to clear and mature, when it is again racked off into wine bottles, which are then corked and cellared.

So long as strict cleanliness is observed in the

kitchen, only innocuous metals used, all vessels and utensils sterilized before use and all water mixed with the juice boiled and cooled, there should be no difficulty in making palatable wines in this way, especially if a good handbook is followed, such as *Making Wine at Home* by Annabelle McIlnay (1974). However, in the last 20 years home wine making has been made more systematic by the use of substances and methods which the reader should know about and follow where practicable.

● **Sugar content of wine.** The maximum alcohol content attainable in any wine is 16–18 percent. (Burgundy contains 10–13 percent, claret 9–11 percent.) The home vintager should as a rule aim at 10–12 percent alcohol in a fruit wine. Since alcohol comes from the sugar present in must, 2 parts fully fermented sugar yielding 1 part by volume alcohol, it is clear that the amount of sugar to be added depends on the quantity of natural sugar in the fruit balanced against the amount of alcohol wanted in the finished wine. To find the sugar content of the fruit juice, you will need a simple instrument called a hydrometer, sold by druggists and wine-makers' suppliers. Pour some of the juice into a measuring cup or tall, narrow jar and find the sugar content by following the printed instructions accompanying the hydrometer. Then use this formula:

Let a = alcohol desired
Let b = percent of sugar found in juice
Let x = percent of sugar to add to juice
Then* $x = 2a - b$. Example:
If $a = 12$ percent
$b = 19$ percent
then $x = (12 \times 2) - 19 = 5$ percent

This indicates that 5 lb. additional sugar will here be required for every 100 lb. crushed fruit or juice, or in other words ½ lb. sugar for every 10 lb. (= 1 1/5 gal.) of fruit or juice.

Sugar is best added to the must in syrup form. Having determined the amount needed, put the sugar in a pan with 2 or 3 pints water and stir while bringing slowly to a boil, skim off any scum, then cover and leave to cool. For a dry wine, just enough sugar should be added for the yeast to ferment it all out into alcohol and gas. More sugar than this would result in a sweet wine, and too much sugar would produce a wine too sickly sweet to drink, in which case refermentation would be necessary.

* The formula is easy to understand if one grasps that the amount of sugar in the juice, b, plus the amount of sugar to be added, x, gives the total amount of sugar to be converted to alcohol, a. If 1 part sugar gave 1 part alcohol, $b + x$ would $= a$. But since it takes 2 parts sugar to make 1 part alcohol, the formula must be adjusted accordingly, and either the total amount of sugar halved, or (which is the same thing) the per cent of alcohol desired doubled to bring the figures into relation.

● **Sterilizing must.** Unwanted molds, bacteria and wild yeasts may be prevented from breeding in the must and tainting the wine if sulphur dioxide (SO_2) is added to the must at an early stage, either in the form of potassium metabisulphite or sodium metabisulphite, ¼ tsp. per gal., or in the form of campden tablets, 2 per gal.

Pectic enzymes if added to the freshly crushed fruit in the proportion of ½ tsp. per 10 lb. fruit, will break down pectin and so reduce haziness in the wine.

Acid or tannin may need to be added to some musts which are insipid or lack astringency. They may be bought in chemical form, or tannin may be extracted by infusion from oak bark or shavings, or from tea, while citric acid is contained in lemon juice and malic acid in apple juice, both of which may be added to musts.

Adding the yeast. Not only the efficient conversion of sugar to alcohol but also much of the bouquet and flavor of the wine depend on the character of the yeast used; some fruits will ferment naturally, but rather than let them do so it is better to wash them in running water and use instead of ordinary yeasts a special wine yeast, of which the all-purpose dried wine yeast is the most convenient. Yeasts will work better very often if a nutrient in the form of dibasic ammonium phosphate, urea, or malt extract is added to the must in the proportion of ½ tsp. per gal.

Instead of adding yeast direct to the must, prepare a yeast starter 2–3 days before making wine by diluting some juice with an equal quantity of water. Heat this to boiling, and cool. Half-fill a sterilized pint bottle with this juice, add the yeast, together with 2 tsp. sugar, and shake. Plug the neck with cotton wool and leave the bottle at room temperature for up to 48 hours. Add this starter to the must in the proportion of ¼ pint per gal. But if as much as, say, 10 gal. wine are to be made, prepare the starter as directed, but instead of adding it direct to the must, add it to a further 2 pints juice in a 1½-quart bottle and allow it to ferment vigorously before adding this larger quantity to the must. For 20 gal., double the quantity.

To make blackberry wine: As the berries wired along your wall become ripe, pick them daily; wash and then crush them and add to the pulping tub or crock with the addition of 3½ pints boiled, warm water to every 7 or 8 lb. of berries, holding back an equal quantity of water for adding later. (Optional procedures are given in square brackets.) [Add campden tablets and pectic enzymes as described.] If a large quantity of wine is to be made it may be as well to have two or more pulping tubs working alternately. Cover the tub or crock with a wad of thick, folded cloth to exclude airborne bacteria and leave for 24 hours after the last input of crushed berries, stirring now and then. Using the legs of a chair upended on the table as a frame, improvise a strainer with a large square of folded muslin and strain the juice from the pulp through this into a bucket or bowl placed on the chair, finally squeezing the pulp hard to extract all the juice. Discard pulp, clean the pulping tub and return the juice to it, adding the rest of the boiled cooled water, to which has been added [the amount of sugar previously calculated by use of the hydrometer and the correct formula or] roughly 2 lb sugar [in the form of syrup] for each 3½ pints. [Using the dried wine yeast or, better still, a special Burgundy yeast], add the yeast starter as described. Cover with a thick cloth and allow the fierce fermentation to proceed for 2 or 3 days. When it subsides, pour the must into casks or jars fitted with fermentation locks, filling them nearly full, and topping up with pure water from time to time as needed. When fermentation ceases, rack off each jar or cask of wine into another sterilized jar or cask, bung it tightly and store in a cool place for 6 months. After that time, again rack off the clear wine into sterilized bottles, corking tightly with corks sterilized by boiling. Store bottles on their sides in a cool shed or cellar for at least 6 months before drinking. Should the wine prior to bottling still be cloudy it may be cleared, or "fined," by the addition of a little isinglass, white sheet gelatine, or white of egg.

Edlerberry wine: Gather the berries when fully ripe, strip them from the stem with a fork, rinse in running water and crush them by hand or in a juice extractor. Follow the procedure for blackberry wine, but use only enough water to equal the volume of juice extracted. Elderberries lack acid, and the wine can be improved by the addition of orange, lemon or apple juice to the must.

Sloe or damson wine: Use only ripe fruit, without stalks. Wash and crush them by hand in a tub without breaking the pits. Follow the procedure for blackberry wine, using about 1 gal. water to every 8 lb. fruit, and about 2 lb. sugar to each gallon of must, but omit citric acid. Elderberries and damsons mixed in the proportions 1 part damsons, 2 parts elderberries, make a palatable wine.

Part V:

MEAT, POULTRY AND DAIRY PRODUCE

□15□

KEEPING GOATS

A. MANAGEMENT

The cow is indispensable on a small farm when the owner has a large family. The farmer can sell surplus milk and butter and feed the skim milk to calves, pigs and poultry. Most cottagers will do better with a pair of goats, which actually produce more milk for food consumed than do cows. The common idea that goats are malign, dirty, omnivorous and smelly is quite wrong. The female goat is a clean and gentle creature, very responsive to affection. Goats are browsers and will eat clean rough stuff that cows would not touch. Their size makes them easy to transport in the back of a car, the caboose of a train or a trailer pulled by a bicycle. Two does, or "nannies," mated in alternate years so that each in turn is allowed to "run on," i.e. give an uninterrupted milk supply for 2 years after kidding, will yield together an average of around 7 pints of milk a day throughout the year. The modern goat is normally hornless. Goats are immune to tuberculosis and seem not to get brucellosis. Their milk is medicinal and can clear up such skin complaints as eczema. Goats do, however, require incessant attention; they cannot be left untended even for a day and must have enough land for their support—about ⅔ acre each. If there is free access to rough grazing, the area required for producing their fodder will be less. Goats do not have to graze at all and may be wholly stall-fed, but will still need grass or alfalfa for hay or silage, some cabbages, kale and winter roots.

● **Needs of goats.** A goat should be housed at night all the year round, and in bad weather. Hay must be supplied in a rack not less than 3 ft. from ground level, and there must be a daily supply of fresh, clean water. Goats should not be tied up when housed, nor should horned goats be penned together. If tethered, a light chain not less than 10 ft. long is needed, with at least two swivels and a light, strong leather collar. The tethering peg must be moved at least twice daily. If tethered during the day, the goat must be free in its shed during the night; if permanently housed, it should never be kept tied up.

Buying a goat. The best goat from a cottager's viewpoint is that which will give the most milk with the least trouble. What is wanted is not a show animal but a strong and healthy goat which can be expected to give about a gallon of milk a day at peak production, if not at her first lactation then at her second or third. Such an animal may be obtained from a recognized breeder or from some isolated farmer who happens to have one or two animals more than he can manage. Choice of breed (whether Toggenburg, French Alpine, Rock Alpine, Saanen or Nubian) will depend largely upon the breeds common in the locality and the presence nearby of a suitable breeding buck or billy of that breed.

● **The breeding cycle.** Lactation occurs when kids are born to the female in the spring, following mating with the buck 5 months previously. In early autumn the doe gives signs that she is "in heat" or "in season" by an intermittent rapid wagging of her tail and a plaintive, insistent bleating; her parts, too, will be inflamed. She should at once be taken for service to the chosen stud male. If the opportunity is missed then, another will occur in 21 days' time, and another 3 weeks after that, and so on, until the mating season is over. If two milch goats are kept, then only one need be sent for service each year, the other if in milk being allowed to run on for another 12 months. This avoids a milkless winter followed by a glut of milk in early summer. The earlier a goat comes into milk the better, so an early mating should be provided for.

A parturient goat will kid without assistance if she is left free of restraint in a pen littered with clean straw or bracken; one, two or three kids may be produced. Examine these at once before they begin to suckle, and destroy any neuter, deformed or male kids not wanted for later eating. If all kids are unwanted males, the mother's attention must be distracted while they are taken away, or she will set up a continual frantic bleating. The mother will need a reviving bucket of bran mash with a spoonful of molasses, or a drink of warm ale. The slippery, mucous afterbirth must be found, wrapped in newspaper and burned; otherwise the goat will eat it. Female kids should be set to the teat as soon as they can stand, for the sake of the valuable colostrum the first milk will contain. Rather than being allowed to run with their mother, taking all the milk they want until they are 3 or 4 months old, they should be given one good feed from the mother and then kept in a separate pen and taught to feed themselves from a bucket of milk, which they will do if first assisted with a dipped finger. There is no need for a bottle. Don't milk the doe right out for the first 3 days after kidding; and instead of cooling and using the milk taken from her, feed it back to her while still warm. It will help her over the strain of kidding and lactation.

At a few days old the kid may be given hay and allowed onto pasture, but it must have milk for 3 months, when the supply may be reduced and some calf meal substituted; at 6 months it should be off milk altogether. Male kids kept for meat must be castrated at 2 or 3 weeks of age. The grown kid or goatling will be ready for mating 18 months from birth, when the best available stud male should be found to improve the breed. Always breed true to type.

● **How to milk.** The milch goat should be trained to step onto a platform raised a foot or more from the ground, where her collar can be fastened to a short tether. The milker sits on a small stool to one side, places a small milking pail on the platform, underneath the goat, and after wiping the udder and its two teats with a clean, damp rag, grasps the teats firmly between the whole of the thumb and all four fingers and applies a successive and continual pressure on the teat, beginning with the first finger near the top of the teat and ending with the little finger nearer the bottom. The whole finger is used, not the tip. First one hand applies the pressure, and then the other, forcing the milk from the constantly filling teat into the 1-gal. stainless steel or tin pail. The foremilk, the first few squirts from each teat, goes into a cup and is thrown away. The goat must be kept calm and relaxed; if she is nervy a satisfactory let-down of milk will not occur. She should be contentedly chewing the cud while being milked. If she kicks, a raised elbow will keep her hind foot from the pail. Before milking is completed, the udder and teats must be stripped of the last vestige of milk. The udder is gently patted and stroked and the teats bumped in imitation of a sucking kid; this fills the teats, and milking is resumed until nothing more will come. This is important—if the goat is not fully milked out her yield will drop from day to day until she dries up. She is now ready to go back to her yard, pen or pasture until her next milking in 12 hours.

The milk must be poured through a filter into a container and cooled by placing the container under the cold tap for 20–30 minutes. The milking pail is first washed with cold water, then scalded and left upside down to drain. Goats' milk is white in color and has a sweet, nutty flavor. Should a musty tang be noticed, it indicates that (a) the milk is not fresh, (b) the utensils used are not sterile or (c) there is something wrong with the goat which needs looking into. Those who have kept goats always prefer goats' milk to cows'. Its cream does not separate so readily, and it is easier to digest.

● **Housing and management.**   If there is no rough

grazing and no meadow grass on which the goats can be turned loose or tethered, then they must be stall-fed with hay and whatever produce you can supply from your own soil. They must have a compound big enough for them to walk about in, containing a small shed for sleeping only—in which case milking will have to be done in a shelter outside the compound—or a large shed containing stalls for four or more goats, a milking parlor and fodder store. For a sleeping shed, a simple, draft-free, rainproof wooden hut will do, or even a hut built up from straw bales cased in wire netting and with a floor of straw litter. A shed as big as a car garage can house four to six goats, and a 6-by-8-ft. lean-to can shelter two or three. A compound must have a 4-ft.-high fence and a secure gate. Goats have an annoying way of squeezing through or jumping over fences and hedges and invading territory where they are not wanted, and they are inclined to strip the bark from garden trees. Every goat enclosure must be really goat proof.

Equipment. Besides a tethering chain with ring, clip and two swivels, goats need an extra strong leather collar, a tethering peg, a plastic or metal drinking pail and one for feeding, a wood or metal indoor hayrack and an outdoor rack for greenstuff, which may also be hung in wide-mesh string bags.

● **Feeding.** Provided the goat can browse and graze freely from May to August or September, all she will need for the rest of the year is a supply of good hay and enough kale and roots for the winter, with some concentrates. Instead of hay she may be fed silage. The preferred roots are cattle beet, which may be fed at any time, and manges, which must be kept until after Christmas when their acid sap turns to sugar. The goat will also consume all sorts of waste garden produce such as turnip and beet tops, Jerusalem artichokes and stalks, cabbage leaves, pea and bean haulm and pods, windfall apples, etc. Hay may be bought by the bale or load, and roots by the ton, from a farmer; but for obvious reasons it is best where possible to grow your own fodder. A 1½-acre plot should suffice for your two milch goats and two kids or one goatling, allowing about ¾ acre for grazing, about ½ acre for hay and ¼ acre for roots, kale and other fodder.

The hay crop. Assuming your grass to be of good quality to start with (otherwise reseeding may be necessary), the time to cut it is while the grass is still young and sappy, and before it has reached the hard-stem flowering stage. The younger the grass the greater its food value, and it is perfectly in order to cut grass as soon as it is 6 in. high and to continue cutting through the summer whenever the grass is long enough to be scythed. This short grass, cut with the scythe, makes a very light swath which begins to dry immediately in conditions where a heavy swath of long grass would dry on top but not underneath. Cutting is done in the morning, the grass raked into rows in the afternoon, then piled and carried to the hay store or stack as soon as it is properly dry. Such short hay packs more tightly and weighs more heavily than long hay, and needs to be fed more sparingly as it is so rich in nourishment. Two fine days together are enough to get such a crop in.

If the hay is cut long, then the swath must be turned two or three times until the hay is fit, that is, until you can wring a bunch of it hard without feeling any moisture, when it can be carted and stacked. If rain threatens before hay is made, the hay should be put into piles which shed water. Rake the hay into large heaps and build them into cone-shaped pikes with pointed tops which will let the rain slide down the outer surface and which will quickly dry out afterwards. Hay makes best on 5-ft. tripods of rough poles drilled and wire-threaded at the top and spread open at the base, over which tripod is slipped horizontally a rough triangle formed of three poles lashed together 12 in. from their ends; this grips the tripod and holds it firm, providing a forked vent at each corner for circulation of air. The hay is piled regularly all around the frame, all loose hay being picked up from the ground at the base so as not to impede the draft of air through the central chimney. Hay so made will be ready in 1–3 weeks but may be left out longer if need be. Rather than building a rick, store the hay under cover—an open-sided, dutch-barn-type shelter is ideal—conveniently near to the goats' compound. Guard against the moist hay heating up and becoming spoiled by giving any dubious hay a wider spread. A few handfuls of salt scattered throughout will absorb moisture and prevent heating.

Making silage. Silage can be a substitute for or a supplement to hay. It is a sort of grass conserve, high in proteins, which can be made without regard to weather conditions. The fresh-cut, wilted grass and other green material is tipped into a circular container and trodden down hard to exclude air. It then heats up, ferments and becomes pickled. Silage may be made in a walled clamp or a well-drained pit lined with straw; but better is an up-ended concrete drain section of, say, 4 ft. across by 6 ft. high, or a structure of about the same size made by bolting together sheets of corrugated iron inside old iron cartwheel tires. Such a silo will hold about 5½ tons of silage made from lawn mowings emptied into it and trodden down hard once or twice a fortnight on a base of 8 in. of straw. (Average yield of grass per acre: 4½ tons; alfalfa: 22½ tons.) Good silage can be made from oats and vetches, alfalfa and chopped kale, as well as sugar-beet tops, the scythed verges of country

lanes, etc., all of which should be wilted before use.
The younger the material the less sugar it will contain; which is why molasses thinned with water (1
gal. molasses per ton of material) is sometimes
added to promote fermentation. The required heat
is 100° F. To tell if the trodden silage is ready for
further filling, push a metal rod into it, and if when
pulled out the next day it is really hot you must
speedily add more stuff; if barely warm, then leave
it for another day. When there is no more material
to include, seal by laying clean sacks on the top and
covering them with chalk. The food value of silage
of 5–7 lb. weight is equal to 1 lb. concentrate or 2
lb. hay or 13 lb. roots.

● **Crops for soiling.** On your spare ¼ acre you
will grow crops for cutting green and feeding to the
goats, with an eye to the barren months of late
winter and early spring. By planning carefully, fam-
iliarizing yourself thoroughly with local climatic and
soil conditions, and taking advantage of the many
varieties of fodder crops, you will be able to provide greenstuff for your animals for much of the
year. Among the most important crops for this
purpose are kale and roots, cabbages, alfalfa, comfrey and chicory.

Other fodders relished by goats are: Jerusalem artichokes, carrots, boiled potatoes, rutabagas, whole
stems of corn, kohlrabi, sugar-beet pulp (soaked),

cut tree branches, bracken, crab apples (halved), elm seeds (fresh or dried), acorns (dried and halved), chestnuts and horse chestnuts (shelled and halved), hazelnuts (unripe, with shells), raspberry canes. Avoid evergreens.

Feeding concentrates. With dairy animals a distinction is made between maintenance and production rations, the first keeping the animal in good health and the second increasing its milk yield. Concentrates serve the second purpose, so never treat them as a main course. Some natural fodders are lacking in certain minerals necessary to the goats' health, and these must be added to food. My own practice has always been to keep a bin of mixed bran, crushed oats and linseed cake (say) and to mix these together with several handfuls of dry seaweed meal. With a bowl of this mixture once a day, before evening milking, my goats have always kept healthy and milked well. Among homegrown concentrates are sunflower seeds, field peas and beans. Goats will sometimes increase their milk yield when given as a food supplement such members of the Umbelliferae family as fennel, caraway and ill. An iodized salt lick is essential.

● **Health of goats.** Goats are hardy, and if well housed, well fed and kept in clean conditions, they should have few health troubles. They should be brushed down hard once a day with a stiff grooming brush, and their hoofs should be examined now and again and pared before the outer horn curves in and overgrows the soft center pad. The knife may be replaced by or supplemented with a file. Dusting with derris powder will get rid of lice and external parasites. Goats can pick up the internal parasites of sheep and should be kept off land that has been grazed by sheep within the last two years. If worm infestation is suspected, feed with carrots for a few days, and if they do not clear the worms, have goat wormed by a vet. If a goat cuts her teat on barbed wire she must still be milked, however deep the gash; use stock iodine on the teat. Paint the whole udder with iodine in cases of udder chills and lumps in the udder. Mastitis needs veterinary attention; milk the goat frequently to prevent the udder becoming full. To treat hoven or bloat, keep the goat moving, massage her stomach, and drench with 3⅓ oz. of bicarbonate of soda to ½ pt. warm water. (To drench a goat, insert a small long-necked bottle in her mouth and tip it upwards at a slight angle.) Should the goat become constipated through wrong feeding or lack of exercise, give her up to 3/5 pt. liquid paraffin. Diarrhea or dysentery is treated by a large dose of liquid paraffin; but it may be a symptom of more serious trouble requiring veterinary aid.

● **Storing milk.** Flow of milk is at its greatest in early summer, while in late winter the flow may be barely enough for daily needs. This unevenness may be leveled by storing surplus summer milk for 6 months upwards in a deep freezer in 1– 2 pint cartons or polythene bags. Do this as soon as the new milk is cooled; if cream rises the milk may separate when thawed. Once thawed, do not refreeze milk.

Milk may be preserved without freezing in corked glass bottles which must be sterile and quite dry. Milk the goat into the bottles and cork them tight as soon as they are filled. Secure the corks with wire. Put the bottles on their bases in a boiler, on straw. Pack straw between the bottles and fill the boiler with cold water. Light the fire or turn on the heat, and when the water begins to boil, remove the heat and let water and bottles gradually cool. When cold, take out the bottles and pack them in sawdust in cartons. Store them in a cool outhouse or cellar. Use within a year.

(One way of sterilizing bottles is to dissolve about 1 oz. caustic soda in 1 qt. cold water, fill the bottles to the brim and let them stand for 30 minutes, then rinse out three times with cold clean water which has first been sterilized by boiling and allowed to cool.)

B. CREAM, BUTTER AND CHEESE

Milk consists of fats, nonfat solids and water. In the making of cream, the fats are separated from the other contents by slow heating. Butter can then be made from this cream; and a superior cheese may be made from cream without the use of a curdling agent. Cheese is more usually made from the whole milk, but a less rich cheese can be made from the separated milk. Cheeses are soft and perishable or hard and keeping according to whether or not they are pressed in a certain manner. Whey, the rejected liquid from cheese, is unpalatable to humans but can be fed to pigs and poultry.

All dairying must be done in antiseptic conditions; utensils must be scalded and sterilized after use, and the milker-dairyman must have clean hands and wear a clean overall in milking shed and kitchen.

● **To scald cream.** Goats' milk separates less readily than cows'. To make Devonshire cream, which will then make butter, pour the whole of two milkings into a shallow pan and allow to stand 24 hours in winter, 12 in summer. Then place the pan over very gentle heat, and leave it until the surface undulations thicken and a ring appears around the pan. Remove the pan to a cool place and skim off cream the next day. To make it into butter, simply beat it up by hand, adding dairy salt.

To make butter from unscalded cream. In this case the cream is ripened (allowed to sour and so develop lactic acid) by skimming it from standing milk and stirring each day's cream into the previous one's, leaving it in a temperature of 56–60° F for several days and adding no cream within 12 hours of making the butter. It should then be velvet-smooth, with a clean acid taste.

You need a simple jar churn (a 1-gal. glass churn with wooden paddles turned by a handle and gear fixed in the lid is best), a pair of wooden "Scotch hands" and a corrugated draining board, all of which must be scalded and stood in cold brine (4/5 lb. salt to 1 gal. water) to prevent sticking. Add cold water to the cream until it resembles emulsion paint. Third- or half-fill the jar and churn it at about 53° F. When the cream begins to thicken add a cupful of cold water and churn some more. The cream will again thicken. Add more cold water and resume churning. Repeat this until the cream breaks into butter grains and buttermilk. Churn again until the grains are firm as rice grains, then wash the butter by pouring cold water into the churn. Churn further, then strain off the liquid through a sieve. Repeat the washing until the water runs away clear. To salt the butter dissolve ½ lb. dairy salt in 5 pints water, pour it into the jar and leave for 10 minutes. Drain off the salt water and pat up the butter with the Scotch hands, pressing out all the water yet not spoiling the butter with overpatting. Good butter keeps over a week in summer, two weeks in winter.

To make cheese. Cheese is a product of the sep-
aration of the fats and solids in milk from the water
(whey) effected by rennet. Special cheese rennet
(not junket rennet) must be bought, and a special
starter to speed the production of lactic acid is also
desirable. You will need some straw mats and some
molds.

(A vegetable rennet may be extracted from the
wild herb called yellow (or lady's) bedstraw. And a
starter may be made at home by (1) milking ½ pint
goats' milk into a sterilized bottle, after a first ½
pint milk has been taken from the goat. Seal the
bottle at once and put it somewhere in a constant
temperature of 80° F. Lactic acid bacteria will multiply and it will become sour. (2) After 3 days take a
similar ½ pint fresh milk in a sterilized bottle and
pasteurize it by standing it in cold water brought
slowly to a boil and kept simmering for 30 minutes.
Cool to lukewarm and pour into it about 1 tsp of
the first soured milk. Seal and place this new mixture in the place of the first bottle, at 80° F, and
leave for 1½ days. This pasteurized soured milk is
the starter you require for making cheese. It may be
replenished by repeating part (2) of the process
every 2 or 3 days, adding a little of the last batch of
soured milk each time.)

A simple press can be made out of a cylindrical
biscuit tin with the lid removed and the bottom perforated, with a slightly smaller and squatter lidded
tin to fit just inside it as a weighted follower, filled

with heavy metal. Put the first tin over a circular wood post and punch some staggered holes in it with a ½-in. nail, then smooth the nail holes inside the tin by hammering it upturned over an iron bar. To use, set the first tin on a rough stand, partly fill with curd, cover curd with a piece of muslin, and place the weighted follower on top.

Soft cottage cheese (1½ lb. from 1 1/5 gal.) can be made from skim milk by letting it go sour and hanging up the thickened liquid in a muslin bag to drain; but this leaves much to chance and makes at best a dull cheese. A better method is to add some lactic acid starter and 1 tsp. diluted rennet extract to 1 1/5 gal. skim milk, to cut the curds when set, heat to 120° F, drain off the whey, and wash the curds in cold water.

Whole milk cheese. For a Neufchâtel type soft cheese, put 1 1/5 gal. sweet whole milk into a pan placed inside a larger pan containing water at 72° F. When the milk reaches 70° F, add 1 tsp. rennet dissolved in 10 tsp. cold water and stir it in. Allow to set overnight. Next day spread a square of clean cheesecloth over a colander and ladle the firm, smooth curd onto it. Tie the ends of the cloth together and hang the bundle up to drain. Stir the curds from time to time, and add some dairy salt. The less whey, the milder the flavor, so press or not as desired. The cheese can be eaten at once.

Try that simple cheese and then compare it with this one, made with a starter. To 1 1/5 gal. fresh milk add 2 tbsp. starter and allow to thicken at 80° F for 20 hours. Mix in 3 or 4 pints fresh milk, then add rennet as above and stand in a cooler place for nearly 12 hours. Strain off the whey and drain the curd. When well drained the curd is ready for use. To make the same without starter a slow setting time of 5–10 hours is needed, and as fresh milk sets quickly it should be allowed to stand at around 80° F for 2 or 3 days before adding rennet; the milk is then kept for 12 hours at 60–70° F until set. Hang it in a bag and treat as above.

Mixed cream and milk cheese. Dilute rennet as described and add it to 1 1/5 gal. milk and cream at 70–80° F. Leave in a cool place to curdle, then tie curds in a cloth as before and hang up in a warm place. Open bag two or three times and turn the curds sides to middle with a knife. The next day stir the contents again and turn into the press under 7 lb. weight for several hours: salt to taste.

Full cream cheese without starter or rennet. Pasteurize the cream by heating it to 150° F, then cool to 65° F, and hang it in a bag as above. Open the bag and stir the cheese every 5 or 6 hours. When nearly set, salt and place in a mold.

To make hard cheese (1 lb. from 1 1/5 gal.). A simple type of hard farmer's cheese that will keep for months when ripe can be made with 1 1/5 gal. milk heated to 85° F, with ⅓ tsp. rennet diluted in 1½ tsp. water. Stir rennet well into the milk for 3 minutes, cover the bowl and leave to thicken. When set, cut the curd into small cubes with a long-bladed knife. Put the bowl in a pan of hot water and heat slowly for 45 minutes to 95° F, stirring gently. Allow the curd to float in the whey for a further 20 minutes, then let it sink to the bottom for 20 minutes more. Drain off the whey and ladle curds into a square of linen scrim cheesecloth and tie into a tight bundle. Leave for 20 minutes, untie bundle and cut the curd into large squares. Tie tightly again and leave for 20 more minutes, then untie and break each piece in half. Tie tightly once again and after yet another 20 minutes break up the curd into pea-sized fragments, adding 2 tsp. dairy salt. Line the mold with a strip of scalded scrim cloth and force the curd in hard. Apply gradually increasing pressure. After 3 hours turn out the cheese, wring out cloth in hot water and return cloth and turned cheese to mold, and press hard. The second day turn the cheese again, but put it in a dry piece of muslin and press hard. On the third day examine the rind, and if smooth and perfect, grease it with lard and bandage with calico to prevent bulging. Put on a wooden shelf and turn every day for 8 weeks to ripen. The finished cheese may be waxed by dipping quickly into 2 lb. beeswax or paraffin wax which has been melted in a double saucepan.

A cheddar-type cheese may be made from pasteurized whole milk. Heat the milk to 80° F, add some starter. Leave for 30–40 minutes, then add enough diluted rennet to curdle the milk. The curd will be set in an hour, when it is cut into small cubes with a long knife and stirred gently while being heated to 100° F. The whey will separate from the curd. Allow to drain for 24 hours. Then turn the curds over and over to induce them to "cheddar," i.e., to combine into a smooth mass. Now cut the cheese into ½-in. strips and add dairy salt. Let the salt blend with the curd, then put it under pressure for 24 hours. Store the solid cheese at 58° F on a wooden shelf for 2 weeks, turning daily. Wipe off any surface mold with a vinegar cloth. At the end of 2 weeks wax the cheese, which will keep for a year if stored at 45° F.

C. YOGURT

Yogurt is a culture of the microbe *Lactobacillus bulgaricus*, which when introduced into milk breeds rapidly at a temperature of 113° F. One needs a small amount of the culture for inoculation, and some means of keeping the inoculated milk at a constant temperature for 6–12 hours. Having once made yogurt, you can continue, using some of the previous batch to start off the next lot, until the bacillus ceases to be effective, when fresh culture must be bought.

Temperature may be kept at 113° F in an ordinary 2-pint thermos, a gallon-sized stainless steel catering vacuum flask, or a lidded bucket or pot placed in a haybox. Lacking these, place the sealed jug of yogurt in a sunny window in summer or near a stove in winter.

Using a double saucepan, bring milk to 113° F, and pour into the previously warmed flask containing a spoonful of yogurt culture; seal and shake the flask. (To make sure that milk is not contaminated by other bacteria, bring it to boiling point and simmer for 30 minutes, then cool to 113° F.) Leave overnight. If the used flask is left unwashed, the yogurt left around the sides after emptying will serve to start off the next day's heated milk. Homemade yogurt, though just as good, will not be as thick as the bought type.

□16□

KEEPING PIGS

The modern cottager who decides to keep a pig should follow in the footsteps of the old-time cottagers and keep, not a breeding sow, who will be more trouble than she is worth, but a weaner, or two weaners bought at 8 weeks old. Two pigs are not much more trouble to keep than one, and they are company for each other. If one is killed and the other sold as a porker at 100–180 lb. live weight, or as a bacon pig at 200 lb., the sale price of the one may go some way towards covering the feeding costs of the other. It takes 7 months to bring a weaner to readiness for slaughter for the cottager's bacon, so that one bought on 1 February will be fit for killing on 1 October, and so on. The flesh will improve in quality if the pig is kept longer, but the high cost of feed usually makes it uneconomical to do so.

● **For and against pigs.** Besides the high cost of their food, pigs have other drawbacks. Unless kept in a well-fenced field, which they will graze, they must have a strongly built sty, which must be put up if you have not one ready-made. Such a sty must be mucked out often and the dung carted to the garden. Pigs must be fed and watered twice a day. They are subject to parasites and diseases and may go sick or die. Having them killed is not exactly pleasant, and there is a good deal of work in coping with the carcass. Then too, one large hog is a lot of flesh and may leave you with more meat on hand than you can well do with.

On the other hand, as the price of pigs varies from year to year, you may have the luck to buy your weaner cheaply. You may be able to get plenty of cheap feed of some sort. You may be able to use a pig or two to root up some rough waste ground and turn it into near cultivable condition. Your land may badly need their dung. And you may have a large, hungry family who will make quick work of two sides of bacon, two hams and all the other pork products. The pros and cons need to be weighed up carefully before you decide whether or not to keep a pig.

● **Housing.** Pigs are kept either (a) indoors in a sty with a sleeping part and a walled yard, or (b) on grassland with a bare wooden or metal ark or a hut built from straw bales. Pigs keep healthier in the open but fatten quicker indoors. A sty, whether of wood, brick or concrete, must be strongly built, with no projections for the pig to gnaw and no points of leverage for his powerful snout. Walls must be smooth for ease of cleaning, and floors must be of nonslip concrete insulated—as to the sleeping part—against cold and damp. This sleeping part should have an insulated roof with some ventilation but no drafts. The yard must be of concrete with a fall of 2 or 3 in. to one corner for drainage, the urine passing through a pipe set in the wall to a brick- or cement-lined sump big enough to hold a large bucket which can be emptied daily onto the compost heap. Straw or other litter is needed for house and yard, and a wood-slat floor or a low bench or bed inside the

Fig. 13

house is desirable. Pigs are clean animals and do not like wallowing in their own muck. A nonoverturnable feeding trough and a bucket for water are all that are needed, except for a block of iodized mineral hung on the wall.

In the field, the pig needs an **A**-shaped wood or metal ark (Fig. 13) with a slatted floor if the ground is inclined to be wet, or a rough hut built from straw bales with a thatched hurdle laid on top. Straw bales measure about 3 by 2 by 1½ in. If the walls are made either 2 or 3 ft. thick, about 30 bales will make a shack large enough for two pigs. It must be wire-netted: that is, either each bale must be wrapped separately in chicken netting or the hut must be finished inside and out with sheep netting; otherwise the pigs will pull the bales to bits. The bottom bales should stand on plastic fertilizer bags or a base of riprap. Instead of bales, thatched hurdles may be used, or stout corner posts fixed in the ground supporting a double skin of wire netting stuffed tightly with wheat straw, the netting being wired at the top to the roof poles. Pigs should not be run on the same grass for longer than one year in case they pick up each others' parasites—which do not, however, affect sheep, geese or cattle. If the grass they eat is of good quality it will account for about 10 percent of their food. A ring through the nose will prevent rooting, but this should not be needed if they get enough rations. Clean water must be provided in a bucket, and food in a galvanized iron trough, unless you feed them cubes which can be strewn on the grass.

● **Food and feeding.** The pig has only one stomach and cannot digest the coarse fodder ruminated by cattle. While pigs will eat roots and greenstuff avidly, as well as forest mast, they have been found to thrive best on meal ground from cereals. The modern standard mixed ration for pigs consists of about 50 percent barley meal, rich in nutritive starch; 35–40 percent middlings, the offal of wheat flour which, besides starch, provides the roughage lacking in barley; and 5–10 percent protein-rich fish meal or soybean meal, together with some minerals. The proportions of each ingredient are varied somewhat with the age of the pig. Ready-mixed meal containing all the pig needs for life and growth may be bought; commercially the easiest way to feed a pig is to give him this meal dry ad lib, with nothing else but clean water, as farmers do. But it takes an average of 3½ lb. of balanced meal mixture to add 1 lb. to the pig's live weight, and a pig bought at 8 weeks will get through as much as 672 lb. of meal before it is ready for killing. Since each meal is costly, and supplies uncertain, you may be forced to cast about for cheaper foods with which to supplement a rather smaller amount of bought meal.

Cobbett, who attempted to reintroduce the corn

plant into England, calling it "Cobbett's Corn," was much in favor of fattening pigs on this corn. Fortunately, the climate of the United States, unlike that of England is well suited to this crop. Corn meal can be used instead of barley, up to 30 percent of the total ration.

Taking barley as the standard against which to measure the value of other foods (apart from cereals), we find that acorns, chestnuts and peas are of the same nutritive value as barley meal, while 1 gal. skim milk equals 1/5 lb. barley meal plus 3/5 lb. fish meal, and 1 gal. whey equals 3/5 barley meal and is high in minerals besides. Cooked potatoes are good food, 1 lb. equaling ¼ lb. barley meal. The following may be taken as a rough guide:

8 lb roots (rutabagas, mangels, beet)
6 lb raw artichokes
12 lb greenstuff (grass mowings,
    cabbages, kale)   } will replace
                                            1 lb. balanced
                                            meal
4 lb cooked potatoes
4 lb good quality kitchen swill

Pigs will eat apples, dried stinging nettles, dried and ground birchbark and bracken roots; they will munch dried acorns and chestnuts, whole or ground into meal, and will grow fat on the mast of beech trees. Of course, there is no need to calculate to the last ounce the value of each bucket of food one gives to a pig, but it is as well to have some idea of what nutriment he is getting and to avoid obvious feeding errors.

On securing your weaner, then, and putting him in the field or in his sty, he need be fed very little for the first week while he settles down and adjusts to new food and conditions. He may then be given meal or pellets in increasing amounts until he is taking all he wants. At 8 weeks a piglet needs feeding four times a day, dropping shortly to three times and then twice daily. As he grows he will eat an increasing amount, from about 2½ lb. a day at 12 weeks to about 7 lb. a day at 24 weeks, this amount then keeping about the same until time for killing.

If fed wholly on meal, the weaner up to about 100 lb. live weight* will need not less than 10 percent protein in the ration, this being cut down to 5 percent after that weight, when fish meal is best replaced by bean or soybean meal. A pig needs roughly 1 lb. meal for every month of his age. The amount fed at weaning, 1¼ lb., needing to be increased by ¼ lb. weekly until 6 lb. a day is reached.

But that is expensive feeding. If meal is to be economized, the normal amount as above can be fed to about 50 lb. live weight and then kept con-

* In the absence of scales a pig's weight may be judged by measuring in inches (a) right round his chest behind the shoulders, and (b) length from between the ears to root of tail. Multiply (a) by (b) and divide by 13, 12 or 11 according to whether the pig is lean, medium or fat. The answer gives the weight in pounds. *Example:* Length 52 in., chest 50 in. $52 \times 50 = 2,600$ in. Assuming a medium fat pig, divide by 12 = 216.8 as approximate weight in pounds. *N.B.* A pig of this weight will give about 155 lb. of meat, as the dead weight is about 72 percent of the live weight.

stant while cheaper foods like potatoes are fed as supplements, 1 lb. of potatoes being added to the ration in place of each additional ¼ lb. meal. After the pig gets to 100 lb., cabbages and roots can be fed on the basis that 1 lb. meal = 10 lb. greens or 8 lb. mangels or rutabagas. (But don't feed mangels or sugar beet before Christmas). Whatever skim milk or whey can be fed will cut down bulk and also enable the pig to digest its present food to better purpose. Be careful not to switch too rapidly from one food to another, upsetting the animal's digestion and appetite, and not to give fresh milk one day and sour the next: better to feed all sour. A healthy pig should be adaptable as to diet, and no doubt if meal were to vanish altogether he could be fattened on potatoes, skim milk, greens, roots and corn, especially if forest nuts were available in the locality for autumn foraging.

● **Killing and curing.** There are regulations covering the humane slaughter of farm animals. For further details, write the GPO for Farmer's Bulletin No. 2138, *Slaughtering, Cutting and Processing Pork on the Farm.* Starving the animal for 24 hours beforehand is essential, but he should be allowed to drink freely.

If killed at home, the pig is secured by a noose around the upper jaw and lifted by two or three men feet upwards onto a strong frame such as a

sawbench, where he is first stunned by a humane
killer or a shot from a .22 rifle held against the head
about ½ in. above the eyes. He is then immediately
stuck with a sharp two-edged knife 6 or 8 in. long
pushed in about 1 in. in front of the breastbone, in
the center line of the body at an angle of 45° to a
depth of about 5 in. towards the heart so that the
main arteries from the heart are cut through. The
heart, undamaged, will continue pumping blood for
some minutes after stunning, and if the arteries are
thoroughly severed, blood will at first fountain from
the knife wound with some force. As the pig bleeds
he is hoisted up by the hind legs to assist in draining the carcass. A block and tackle rigged up at a
height of 10 ft. will assist in this, or the pig's hind
legs may be shackled and the pig hoisted by them
before sticking. Again, the pig can be killed on the
ground, one man standing astride him grasping the
forefeet and preventing the body from rolling with
his legs while the other stuns the animal and
pushes in the knife.

The carcass is either scalded in hot water at 140–
150° F to loosen its hair and scurf, after which it is
scraped smooth with a blunt knife; or it is scorched
and scraped. Cobbet advises that the hair of the pig
be burnt rather than scalded. "As the hair is to be
burnt off it must be dry, and care must be taken
that the hog be kept on dry litter of some sort the
day previous to killing. When killed he is laid upon
a narrow bed of straw, not wider than his carcass,

and only two or three inches thick. He is then covered all over thinly with straw, to which according as the wind may be, the fire is put at one end. As the straw burns, it burns the hair. It requires two or three coverings and burnings, and care is taken that the skin be not in any part burnt, or parched. When the hair is all burnt off close, the hog is scraped clean, but never touched with water. The upper side being finished the hog is turned over, and the other side is treated in like manner. This work should always be done before daylight, for in the daylight you cannot so nicely discover whether the hair be sufficiently burnt off. The light of the fire is weakened by that of the day." The straw may be helped out with dry newspapers held as torches.

The next step is to cut open the scraped carcass and remove the innards or offal. The body cavity is then washed with cold water and the carcass sawed in two through the center of the backbone, and the head cut off. It is hung up to chill, but not to freeze, for 24–28 hours, after which it is cut up as required. Nearly all the parts of a pig are edible if prepared in the proper way, but there is a good deal of kitchen work involved in rendering the fat into lard, making brawn from the head and hocks, mincing spleen fillets and trimmings into sausages, etc. The owner of a deep freezer will have no problem in storing pork. Others will have to hang fresh meat, lightly covered with bran or powdered borax,

in a room or passage where there is a cool current
of air, pickling the rest in brine until wanted for
later soaking and boiling. The two flitches and
hams will of course be salt-cured and dried or
smoked.

● **Curing bacon and ham.** For curing, 1 lb. dry
salt is needed for every 10 lb. meat; and to this is
now usually added ¼ lb. fine powdered saltpeter
for every 10 lb. salt, and some brown sugar. The
first step is to soak all the pieces of meat to be
cured in a cleansing brine made up with 13 lb. salt
mixed with 4 oz. saltpeter in 6 gal. hot water.
Allow the water to cool, and put in the meat. After
1 hour take out the meat and let the brine drain off.
Then lay the two flitches on a bench and into the
flesh side of each rub the curing mixture of salt,
sugar and saltpeter. Treat the hams and other
pieces in the same way. Do this in a cool, stone-
floored room if possible, at about 40° F. Next make
a 2-in.-thick bed of salt and press flitches and hams
into it skin side down, and lightly sprinkle with the
curing mixture of salt, sugar and saltpeter. Cover
them all with 2 in. salt, packing it tightly around
them. Leave for 5 days; take off the stale salt; dust
the flitches and hams with curing mixture again,
and again pack down in fresh salt. Do not leave for
longer than 5 weeks. Remove flitches and hams,
scrape off the salt and wipe the surfaces as dry as

possible. Hang them up from hooks in the ceiling at room temperature until fully dry. When dry, wrap in muslin or calico against flies, and hang up in a cool place.

● **Smoking bacon and hams.** Bacon that is only salted and dried is green bacon. It is perfectly good, but some people prefer bacon to be smoked. To smoke it, instead of hanging the flitches from the ceiling, hang them in the open chimney over a wood fire, having first laid them on the floor and liberally strewn and patted bran or fine sawdust upon the flesh sides to keep the flesh clean. Don't burn peat or coal on the fire, nor any pine, fir or larch wood. With a constant wood fire, the flitches will be dried in about a month; they should be quite dry but not dried out and rigid. They must not hang so low that the flames melt them, and they must not be wet by rain coming down the chimney.

In the absence of an open chimney indoors, a smokehouse can be improvised from a small out-door shed, to which the smoke from a brick-lined underground firebox is led by a drainpipe passing under one wall of the shed and up through the floor, the flitches being hung on hooks from a bar placed across the shed near the roof. Hams, being smaller, can be smoked in an empty hogshead. Near the bottom of the barrel drill two holes and

through them push a section of broomstick from
which to hang the hams. Near the top, cut a hole in
the side through which to insert an iron pan filled
with sawdust and pieces of green stick. Turn the
barrel upside down, hang the hams upon the
cross-stick, push the iron pan into the opening, put
a chunk of red-hot metal in the pan and cover it
with oak sawdust, and the barrel will quickly fill
with thick smoke. Renew the fuel from time to time
and leave the ham to smoke for about 40 hours.

Alternatively (Fig. 14), place your hogshead right
side up on the ground, having first cut a round
hole in the bottom for the entrance of smoke.
About 12 ft. away from the barrel dig a fire pit,
with a trench sloping upwards from the pit to the
barrel, and either covered with a 12-ft. piece of

Fig. 14

wide planking or lined with pipes or tiles. Fill in some earth around the base of the barrel and over the top of the board or pipes. Hang the hams from a broom handle resting in grooves in the top of the barrel, and over it place a wooden cover. Now light a fire of oak sticks and billets in the pit, and cover it with a metal plate which can be propped open for intake of air. Add fuel as needed, and smoke hams for about 40 hours.

Smoked or dried hams are best stored away in a chest or box filled with dry, sifted wood ashes where neither flies nor air can penetrate, and kept in a dry place. They will keep for more than a year in this way.

□17□

KEEPING HENS

When eggs are cheap and plentiful, as they were for a time under farm-factory production methods, little or no money is saved by keeping one's own hens. But one can have the satisfaction of raising fine, healthy fowls (which those in commercial hen batteries are not) and obtaining eggs full of nourishment and flavor, and, it may be, conserving some valuable pure strain of stock against the time when the factory system breaks down and the breeders of low-consumption, high-production hybrids go out of business. Hens will lay an egg a day each when in production, breaking off only in the autumn molting period when they renew their feathers, and when they go broody. They eat about 4 oz. of food a day and return about 112 lb. each of valuable manure a year to the gardener. They are by no means immune from pests and diseases, but these may be kept at bay by air, sun, exercise, right feeding and clean housing.

Hens require management. You cannot buy a dozen fowls, put them behind netting in an odd corner, feed them and leave the rest to chance. They must be well housed and have plenty of living space. A grass run will soon become a patch of mud unless it provides upwards of 25 sq. yd. grass for each bird. It is unprofitable to keep a bird beyond its second laying season. A chick hatched in February or March will begin laying, as a pullet, the following autumn; she will continue through the winter and on to the end of the next summer as a hen; but in the second winter there will be few eggs, and only one out of two hens will lay steadily through the second year. For this reason, poultry keepers who know their job get rid of half the birds before autumn and replace them with young pullets. So there must be room and housing both for the laying flock and for each year's batch of new pullets.

Pullets will come into lay without the stimulus of a male bird, laying ordinary infertile eggs. A cockerel eats extra food, is noisy and fierce; so most people keep a few hens only, and make replacements each spring with bought day-old chicks, usually hybrids. There is much satisfaction, however, in keeping a cock and breeding one's own birds, not hybrids but purebred stock. The advantage of purebred birds is that if you have, say, one cock and six hens, they will breed true, which means that you may be sure of having in future years birds of exactly the same type as you begin with now. These birds will reproduce themselves, so that there will be no need for the annual buying-in of hybrid chicks from breeders. If you choose a heavy breed such as the White Rock, you will have birds equally good for egg production and for meat, and hens which will with no trouble to you hatch their own brood of chicks each season from their own clutch of eggs and raise them to the stage at which they can leave her and fend for themselves. The light breeds do not go broody so readily.

If you want to breed, but prefer a mixture of two distinct stocks (it may be purebred Rhode Island Red cockerels mated with purebred Barred Plymouth Rock pullets, or vice versa), you will have the first-year benefit of "hybrid vigor"; but if you then continue to breed from within the flock, the features obtained in the first cross will vanish and you will end with a mongrel flock which will have lost all distinctive appearance and be valueless for sale as breeding stock. Since mongrels of any sort need as much food and attention as purebreds, it is surely better to have the latter in the long run. Excessive inbreeding may be avoided by swapping cockerels at intervals with other owners of the breed. The activities of commercial breeders have resulted in the near extinction of the pure breeds today, so the small man who specializes in one of them may be rendering a service to future generations of mankind. Some of the most popular pure breeds and varieties in the United States are: Rhode Island Red, Light Brahma, Brown Leghorn, White Leghorn, New Hampshire Red, Buff Plymouth Rock, Jersey Giant, Barred Plymouth Rock, White, Black and Buff Minorca, White and Buff Orpington.

● **Housing and equipment.** The trend in poultry keeping throughout the last 30 years has been from free range to semi-intensive to intensive methods in which the birds are confined separately in small wire cages under artificial light—concentration camps for hens. With higher wages and the super-market culture, working men have given up their backyard poultry houses, so that henhouses of the old type have gone off the market. They can some-times be picked up secondhand, in poor condition; but one may be forced to make one's own housing. Plans for houses can be found in old books on poultry keeping and old household encyclopedias. Pick one of these and sketch it out on paper, with whatever modifications and simplifications you de-sire. To build it, visit first a secondhand timber and junkyard, where doors, floors and windows can be obtained cheaply, as well as useful timber sections and boarding. Cheap new materials are: plywood, hardboard, matchboard for walls; welded mesh for floor; clear rigid plastic, which can be cut for win-dows and skylight, and linoleum and tarred felt for the roof.

Allow more space than you think you will need: if you intend to keep ten hens, make a house big enough for twenty. It is best to construct a frame of 2-by-2-in. timber, making each side separately and then bolting them together, cladding this frame with outdoor hardboard, asbestos board or plywood, leaving spaces for windows, a pophole for the birds to use and a door for human access to the inside. The floor can be of wood slats (for the dung to drop through), expanded metal or welded mesh from a builder's merchant, but not wire netting. A wood or metal tray slid under the floor makes it easy to remove the droppings for dry storage.

A weather-, rat- and foxproof house should be aimed at. The door at the front must fit exactly and have a lock. The pophole at the left-hand end has to be kept shut at night with a board which slides up and down within two holding strips of batten, being hooked up by a wire or chain during the day. Make your perches of 2-by-2-in. timber with top edges slightly rounded for the hens' claws to grip, and set them lengthwise inside the house, resting at each end in squared sockets. The house should be draftproof, but with a space for air at the top angle of the roof. All wood, inside and out, should be well creosoted on completion, and once a year thereafter, an important sanitary measure. Foxes will be put off by a flat metal boot-scraper with vertical bars laid in front of the pophole and by loose tins containing marbles which rattle at a touch, hung from the netting. If a nest box is included in the house, it must be arranged so that eggs can be taken from outside the house.

For pullets, an **A**-shaped ark without perches, with a slatted floor, an opening at one end and a roof that lifts up is all that is needed.

For feed, the best container is a 100-lb.-size outdoor hopper of galvanized metal; the conical top is lifted off, the bag of meal, pellets or grain dumped into the vessel, sufficient for several weeks, and the top replaced. The feed will trickle into the circular trough at the base a little at a time as the hens peck it out. A large galvanized water container of a similar type, which releases water as it is drunk, is also needed where there is no means of supplying water continuously from a pipe. The birds' need for a dry dust or ash bath should also be provided for.

Placing of henhouse.   Poultry do well if encouraged when chicks to eat grass; if not so encouraged, they may never learn to graze. If there is no grassed orchard, consider fencing off an area of garden with wire netting or, better, chain link fencing, setting the house in the center of one side and dividing the enclosure down the middle so that it is just included in one of the two sections. Allow the hens to run freely on one side while the other is dug and planted with a leaf crop such as alfalfa or a sward of clover and mixed grasses. In the autumn,

move the netting a few feet so that the house is
now in the grassed section, letting the birds run on
it through the next year while cultivation is done in
the section which the hens have scratched, dunged
and rid of pests. This alternation carries on from
year to year. It permits a hay crop to be taken from
one side while the other is occupied. Or the unused
side can be dug for a vegetable crop. The hens will
benefit if a rough shelter is set up in a corner of
each yard, with a floor of litter, to serve as a
scratching shed in wet weather. Nest boxes, which
need not have individual compartments, can be set
up here.

● **Hatching chicks.**   A small flock of birds may be
started by borrowing a broody hen from a poultry-
keeping neighbor, who will be glad to lend one or
two to save the cost of feeding, and giving her (the
hen) either a doz.en day-old chicks or a dozen fertile eggs of the chosen breed. Don't invest in expensive brood equipment: a broody hen is far more
efficient than any infrared lamp or other gadget,
however expensive. If you give her eggs to hatch
out, let them be 2 oz. or slightly over in weight,
rather oval in shape and of strong and smooth shell
texture. Test for fertility by holding each egg
against a lighted lamp, rejecting any which are
blemished. Allow for the loss of one or two in
hatching.

Make a simple coop without a bottom to it out of a 2-ft.-sq. box. Cover the roof with waterproof material, and make the front of vertical slats, two of which can be pulled up to make an exit for the hen, for while sitting she must be allowed to exercise herself once or twice a day, to void herself and to take nourishment. Then make a floor over which the box is to be put by cutting two turfs of the right size, sandwiching the soil sides together, and putting them on the ground where the hen is to sit. The earth between the two sods of grass must be kept damp, the moist warmth resulting from the heat of the hen's body combining with the dampness in the turf being necessary for successful hatching. Put the hen in the coop in the afternoon and let her settle comfortably. After nightfall, gently place the eggs under her one by one; she will receive, shuffle and arrange them herself. As soon as the chicks emerge on the nineteenth day, pull out the brittle bits of shell from under the hen, if you wish, but don't otherwise disturb her.

Care of chicks.   Chicks need frequent feeding. A first feed may be made up from chopped hard-boiled egg with some minced greenstuff sprinkled on a flat feeding board pushed into the coop, with a saucer of milk. Repeat this two or three times before giving them commercial chick crumbs and water. They will soon leave the coop and peck about in the short grass on their own. Put their feed in a galvanized metal chick trough where they cannot foul it by standing on it, and give them a pint-sized water fount which they cannot get into. Cull out any weakly, sickly or deformed chicks at once. Cull again in 2 weeks, taking out any chicks which are not clean, bright, alert and active. Further culling must be done at 5 or 6 weeks, again at 3 months, and again if necessary when the birds reach the point of laying. There is no point in keeping third-rate fowls.

As the chicks grow they will take coarser food, with larger gaps between feeds. After a few days let them run about freely with their foster mother, who will protect and warm them, scratch for them, and teach them how to behave. Take the mother away at 8 weeks, leaving the growing chicks undisturbed. Instead of a coop they should now have a slat-floored ark. At 12 weeks separate the cockerels from the pullets, putting them in a separate enclosure from which they can be taken for killing as needed or sent to market at about 4 months of age.

● **Feeding.** In normal times ready-mixed foods in the form of mash, pellets or crumbs are obtainable from the big milling combines who deliver at weekly or fortnightly intervals. These mixes contain all the bird needs, apart from water and greenstuff, but they are expensive. You may prefer to buy chick crumbs or starting mash for your chicks, gradually replacing it with an all-mash growing ration or a combination of growing mash and cracked grain. At 15 weeks the birds may be fed with equal parts of mash and grain—wheat, oats, barley or corn—in which case the birds must have a constant supply of flint grit to help them grind the grain in their crops. Laying birds also need oyster shell or limestone grit to make their shells. Put these in separate open tins.

One expert, Jim Worthington, in his *Poultry-Keeping Simplified* (1964), has shown that if laying birds are given nothing but grain and fish or meat meal in such a way that they can always help themselves, and provided they can get at natural herbage and earth as well as water, they will select just the quantity of each foodstuff that they need, without wastage. He points out that a cheap bulk feeder can be made by filling a clean 5- or 10-gal. oil drum with grain, putting back the "lid" which one has previously drilled off, and knocking out with chisel and hammer a circle of small gashes all the way round the base of the drum just big enough for the grains to show through so that they can be pecked out. The drum is hung from a branch just above beak level so that the hens have to hop upwards each time they peck. Fish meal is costly, and if hard to get, then soybean and other protein-rich meals might be tried.

If you keep only half a dozen layers, they can be fed on household scraps, potatoes and other surplus vegetables, and whey saved from cheese or butter making, boiled up in a pan and dried off with meal. This mash could be fed once a day, and a second feed given of grain. It is a mistake to keep more fowls than you need for egg production in the hope of selling your surplus eggs—unless, that is, you have an arrangement with a neighbor to exchange your eggs for his bacon, milk or cheese.

Garden crops for poultry. It is not difficult to grow a patch of wheat, rye or oats in an odd quarter acre, broadcasting the seed, harrowing it in, then harvesting the grain by hand in the old way by cutting off the ripe ears with a sickle. No need to thresh; the ears being dry, husk will not rot the grain. Store the heads in sacks inside metal bins and feed the birds by throwing them a few handfuls at a time, in litter, where they will have to scratch for the grain. If you plant corn, it should be field corn. Leave the cobs on the plant until ripe, then husk them, hang them up in bunches under shelter to dry, and store in bins. The stems and foliage are relished by goats.

Sunflowers are valuable. After flowering, cut off a complete disc with its mass of black, oily seeds and toss it to the birds to peck at. Don't store sunflower heads; they will rot the seeds. Spread them out in the sun, face down on a wire netting rack with newspapers underneath to catch the seeds. Store seeds in bins or jars. These seeds have a moist white kernel which can be eaten raw by humans or used in cooking.

Russian comfrey makes good summer feed, its high protein content allowing a small reduction in the amount of fish meal fed to birds.

Cabbages and kale for poultry can be grown all the year round. Tie the whole plant to a frame or branch so that the birds have to hop up to peck at it, for they will waste leaves thrown on the ground.

Beans, carrots, parsnips, peas, rutabagas and turnips can all be fed to poultry, dried peas being fed as grain, dried beans being soaked and minced, carrots and turnips being sliced and hung up raw or, like parsnips, cooked and added to mash. Poultry will eat windfall apples to excess if allowed. They will eat stinging nettles if these are first cut and wilted, the seeds being particularly liked.

A bunch of tansy, rue or mint hung in the hen house will keep flies away.

● **Killing poultry.** The selected bird should be starved for 24 hours, to empty stomach and bowel. Hold the bird by the feet in the left hand, gathering up the wing tips in the same hand. Take hold of the head with the right hand so that its comb lies in the palm, and extend the neck to its fullest extent, keeping up this pressure, bending the hand inwards towards the wrist until the neck "gives," when the bird will convulse and flap its wings (if they are not held) with decreasing violence. Let the bird hang head down; its eyes will close and wings hang loose. Hang it from a branch or beam so that the blood will drain into the space in the dislocated neck. Pluck feathers while the carcass is still warm. The method is the same for killing ducks. If your wrist is weak use the ground-bar method adopted for killing geese and turkeys. A ground bar is a 2½-ft.-long piece of wood with a notch shaved out in the center about 1 in. deep and 6 in. long. The bar is laid on the ground with the notch over the bird's neck, comb upwards. Holding the bird's feet in the right hand, with its breast towards you, and placing your feet one on each end of the bar, you dislocate the neck with a steady pull, the sudden "give" telling you when the neck is broken.

● **Preserving eggs.** Eggs will retain their freshness for some weeks if placed small end downwards in holed racks or shelves in a cool cellar. To preserve a glut of summer eggs for the winter months, drop them into a solution of waterglass (sodium or potassium silicate) in a large crock or galvanized pail containing a wire mesh liner which can be pulled up when the eggs are wanted. A substitute for waterglass can be made by mixing together in a tub 1 bushel quicklime, 2 lb. salt, and ½ lb. cream of tartar with as much water as is needed to bring it to a consistency in which an egg will barely float. Eggs may also be preserved by coating their shells with gum arabic, afterwards packing them in dry charcoal dust. A very old method is to take eggs warm from the nest, grease them with butter or lard and pack them in boxes between layers of bran.

☐18☐

KEEPING GEESE

The salient facts about geese are (1) that their profitable life is several times as long as that of other fowls. The same pen can be kept for 10 or more years, the geese keeping up the same rate of egg and gosling production throughout. Then (2), with some meadow grass they are quite the cheapest bird to keep, for they are close grazers and will thrive upon grass, weeds and garden stuff with one meal a day of scraps and mash for egg production. One acre of meadow will support 15 grazing geese. (3) They are even easier to house than ducks and may be kept in a rough hut made of sods on three sides with a rough thatch roof, or with no house at all if there is no danger from predators. Unlike ducks, they lay their eggs in one place, under a hedge or in their shelter, which should have a floor of clean litter.

Goslings may be reared by putting the eggs

under hens; but a breeding hen will begin laying early in the spring, when one of the geese will soon show signs of broodiness. She will lay her clutch of eggs in a corner and sit on them for 28–30 days until they hatch, behaving afterwards just as a hen does with her chicks except that she will be an even more fearless protector of her brood. A hen can manage only four goose eggs, but a goose will sit on thirteen or fourteen. A breeding pen of three geese and a gander will produce about a hundred fertile eggs in a year.

Feed the goslings for 2 or 3 days on chopped hard-boiled egg and biscuit meal moistened with water or skim milk; then leave out the egg and get them gradually used to a simple wet mash fed two or three times a day, reducing this after 9 weeks as they are able to eat the short grass. It is widely believed that swimming water is needed if geese are to lay fertile eggs, but I have not observed this to be the case; but they must have drinking water at all times. A cross between a young Chinese gander and a yearling Embden goose yields a good bird for eating, but you may not have much choice of breeds locally.

One word of warning: if kept in an open situation, geese are liable to stretch their wings in a high wind and soar away. To forestall this, have the flight feathers of one wing clipped now and then with the shears.

Another warning: geese are tough birds to kill.

□19□

KEEPING DUCKS, GUINEA FOWL & PIGEONS

A. DUCKS

If you keep hens you will not need ducks; if ducks, hens will be superfluous—it is false economy to keep both. On balance, I think hens are preferable, but there are some situations which are ideal for ducks when, and if you like their eggs, it would be folly not to keep them. The eggs are larger than hens', with shells of a smoother grain, usually of a glaucous tinge; their whites are more glutinous. Ducks are hardy and suffer from few diseases, and a good Khaki Campbell female will lay in a year up to three hundred eggs. They are easy to house, since they will do without shelter altogether; but it is best to give them a bare, perchless hut which can be shut at night—and which should be kept fastened until about 9 A.M. the next day, to give them

time to lay their eggs all in one place. Unlike hens
they lay always first thing in the morning, and if let
out too early will drop their eggs wherever they
happen to be standing or swimming. Ducks are
muckier than hens but appear cleaner because of
their water habits. Their droppings are more noisome, and their large webbed feet cause them to
puddle the earth into mire whenever they are confined to a small area in wet conditions: they need
each at least 12 sq. ft. of room. If they are kept near
the house, their voluble quacking can get on one's
nerves and annoy neighbors. They tend to wander:
I have in two separate holdings kept ducks near a
stream, and they would invariably sail away after
breakfast, only returning for their evening feed,
having traveled quite long distances in quest of
wild tidbits from stream and bank.

The most common breed in America is the White
Pekin, a good meat source but a poor sitter with a
short laying season. The Aylesbury, an English
breed, is similar and less high-strung, but harder to
find. The Khaki Campbell and Indian Runner are
prolific egg layers but a bit lightweight for table
purposes.

● **To raise ducklings.**   Buy a clutch of fertile eggs
of the preferred breed and place them under a
broody hen in a coop. The hen will treat them

when hatched as her own progeny but should be taken away when they are big enough to protect themselves and find their own food. If you want fertile eggs for further breeding, keep one drake to six or eight ducks.

Feeding. The ducklings can be fed on chick crumbs or breadcrumbs moistened with sour milk or finely minced household scraps, until they are ready to eat an ordinary layer's mash ration like that fed to fowls, except that it must be damp but not sloppy. A circular feeding trough can be made from a car tire sliced in half. Ducks will do well on a mash of boiled potatoes and meat scraps, with brain or crushed grain. The lighter-feeding breeds may simply be tossed a few handfuls of bread scraps and corn. Ducks do not graze but will eat greenstuff thrown to them, particularly the lighter-leaved plants like lettuce and comfrey. Cobbett used to feed his ducks on "grass, corn, white cabbages and lettuces, and especially buckwheat, cut, when half ripe, and flung down in the haulm." When he wanted to fatten them, he put them in a clean pen, where they could get at no filth, and fed them on oats, cabbages, lettuces and water.

Water for swimming is not essential for ducks, and many believe, with Cobbett, that it does them positive harm. This may be so with foul and stagnant water, but I cannot believe that clean running

water does them anything but good. They must
have at least enough water to wet their feet, which
otherwise will become cracked and calloused.

Ducks are invaluable in clearing slugs from a garden, but do not let them in until they have break-
fasted, or the quantity of worms and slugs they eat
may make them ill; their long bills, too, will make
short work of a row of lettuce.

Ducks are killed, plucked, drawn and cooked in
much the same way as hens.

B. GUINEA FOWL

In a household where not many eggs are eaten, the
guinea fowl, an African bird of the pheasant family,
may be kept for its flesh, which is excellent in a
gamy way, and the occasional rich and delicate
hard-shelled egg. Guinea fowls are hardy, require
no housing at all (they roost in the trees), and fend
for themselves, requiring only some supplementary
feed in the winter. The best way to secure a stock is
to get a sitting of eggs and hatch them out under
an ordinary hen. Keep the chicks in a run with
their foster mother for the first 3 weeks, feeding
them as ordinary chicks, with six meals a day for
the first month, dropping to four meals a day for
two weeks and three meals a day for the next 6
weeks. If left alone (killing all but one of the cocks
as required for the table) they will rear the next and

subsequent generations themselves. Guinea fowl are quarrelsome and are best not kept with other poultry. When alarmed, they make a peculiar high-pitched call, and are sometimes kept on lonely farms to give warning of the approach of strangers.

C. PIGEONS

The pigeon lofts seen at the tops of stone barns in old farmsteads were put there for breeding pairs who would feed themselves on farm leavings without trouble to their owners, who kept them for the squabs, the tender 4-week-old birds without the muscular wing development which makes older pigeons too tough to eat except in stews. As a pair of pigeons will consume more than 100 lb. grain per year, this makes the ten or twelve squabs they will produce rather costly if the grain has to be bought.

But if there is a lot of free food around, it might pay to buy a pair of one of the well-fleshed breeds like the Red Carneaux, the Giant Homer, or the White or Silver King, allowing them to fly free and housing them in a shed where the squabs are easily taken from the nests when required for pigeon pie, and where the valuable pigeon dung can be caught and collected in a droppings pit or tray littered with sawdust or peat and stored for use on compost heap and garden. Pigeons breed from February to July, laying two eggs at a time which incubate in 18 days. The breeds mentioned produce squabs weighing 14–28 oz. at 25–35 days old. The standard pigeon feed is an equal mixture of maple peas, tares, durra, beans and broken maize.

□20□

RABBIT KEEPING

Rabbits are kept for their meat; but as the skins of some breeds are valuable, it is wise when choosing a breed to pick a dual-purpose animal such as the chinchilla, the flesh of which can be eaten and the pelts dried and sold.

Consider at the outset how many carcasses you will need throughout the year and then keep the right number of does—up to twelve—to go with the one buck you will need for breeding. Does can breed at 7 or 8 months, with a first mating in early February. There is a 30-day gestation period, with a litter at kindling of five to eight young. The doe can be mated again in 5 or 6 weeks. At this rate she will produce say five litters a year, or thirty rabbits. Three does and a buck will produce ninety rabbits. If killed at 4 lb. live weight, which produces a dead weight carcass of 2¾ lb., they will provide up to 200 lb. of meat in the year, or nearly 4 lb. of meat a week, together with the ninety pelts. In this time they will have gone through a lot of food, since a rabbit eats daily about 2 oz. per lb. of its weight. Be sure, then, that you will have enough hay, roots and greenstuff to feed this number of rabbits as well as any other livestock.

● **Housing.** Rabbits will thrive in hutches under shelter, but much of the work of attending to them can be saved by running instead an outdoor colony surrounded by 5-ft.-high wire netting of 1-in. mesh, sunk at the bottom 18 in. or more below soil level to prevent burrowing. Each rabbit needs at least 6 sq. ft. of space, with access to indoor breeding and sleeping quarters. If they can be given an area of about 10 sq. ft. in a barn or a large shed with an earth floor, fiberglass or other barriers being sunk 18 in. into the soil, then the work of clearing out their droppings daily can be saved by having a compost pit in the floor. Dig the pit 3 ft. deep and fill it with compostable materials and activator; let it heat up and decompose, and then add as many earthworms as you can find. The rabbit droppings will be composted as they fall and are trodden in, making a useful manure which need be removed only once a year. Put a bale of straw in the corner for nest-making material, and cut a small door so that the rabbits can pass in and out to the feeding area.

● **Feeding.** Rabbits are fed mainly on mixed greenstuff and kitchen mash in summer, and on kale, roots, hay and mash in winter. Cereals are desirable but not essential; whole oats are the best. Cooked potatoes dried off with bran make a good cheap mash, and barley straw can be fed in winter instead of the costlier hay. Rabbits should have as varied a diet as possible; they should have a block of mineralized salt to lick, as well as water at all times. Suitable wild and cultivated foods are:

Cultivated

Jerusalem artichokes	beets	brussels sprouts
cabbages	carrots	cauliflower
celery	clovers	dandelion
kales	kohlrabi	lettuce
alfalfa	mangles	parsley
pea haulm	parsnips	sainfoin
spinach	sunflower seeds	rutabagas

Wild

agrimony	bramble	burnet
carrot, wild	clovers	coltsfoot
common comfrey	cow parsnip	cleavers (goose grass)
chickweed	crosswort	dandelion
dock	goutweed	groundsel
hawkweed	hedge parsley	ivy
knotgrass	mallow	nipplewort
plantain	shepherd's purse	sow thistle
trefoil	vetch	watercress
yarrow		

The fenced outdoor area will provide much of the feed the rabbits need in summer and autumn if it is sown with a grass and clover sward—which they will nibble to a close turf—with Russian comfrey and/or giant chicory planted out at 3-ft. centers. A miniature garden pond will give drinking water, and partial shade can be provided by a suitable bush or tree. The rabbits can then be left to breed naturally, but the buck must be watched and removed to a separate pen if he is troublesome. Butchering of the young rabbits can begin from 8 weeks old. See pp. 229-231.

Pelts are dried by simply nailing them on boards left in the open air. Pack them flat in pairs, skin to skin, with a sprinkling of dried herbs or of flaked naphthalene to keep away moths. Making them into furs is a craft that can be learned, but it is usual to send them away for curing to specialist firms.

Part VI:

WILD FOODS

□21□

WILD ANIMALS FOR FOOD

In giving the following account of the wild animals in the United States which may be killed and used as food it is not my intention to encourage the indiscriminate slaughter of wild animals but to give the reader information on the subject which it is assumed he will make use of only at time of real need.

Game laws. The taking of animals, birds and fish is largely regulated by the individual states, though there are some federal guidelines, mainly pertaining to migratory birds and endangered species. Consequently, game laws vary widely from place to place. Some species are protected and may be hunted, if at all, only within strict limits. The open season (the period of time during which hunting or fishing is authorized) may range from a few days to almost year-round, depending on quarry and location; or the season may be closed altogether for a particular species in any given year. There may also be bag and catch limits and seasonal variations in shooting and fishing hours. Hunting and fishing licenses are generally required by all states, and special permits may be necessary for the taking of certain species. Most regulations apply both to public and private lands, and it is wise to consult the department of conservation in your state for details (see Appendix).

● **Game animals and birds** of the United States may be divided into four categories: upland game, waterfowl, big game and varmints. The following lists give the general distribution of the more common or sought-after animals and birds which may be fair game in certain places at certain times.

Upland game
Mourning dove (nationwide)
White-winged dove (southernmost states, east to west)
Dusky grouse (western mountain regions)
Franklin's grouse (northwest)
Ruffed grouse (northerly states, east to west)
Sage grouse (northwest)
Sharp-tailed grouse (northwest)
Chukar partridge (west of Rockies)
Hungarian partridge (northern states west of New York)

Ring-necked pheasant (northern states)
Prairie chicken (midwest to eastern Colorado)
Ptarmigan (west)
Bobwhite (midwest and east)
California quail (Pacific coast)
Gambel's quail (southwest)
Wild turkey (nationwide)
Woodcock (east of Mississippi River)
Cottontail rabbit (nationwide)
Snowshoe rabbit (north-central and northeast)
Fox squirrel (mid-Atlantic, southeast, south-central)
Gray squirrel (midwest, east)

Waterfowl

Ducks (more than twenty widely distributed species)
Geese (some half-dozen widely distributed species)
Shorebirds (cranes, gallinules, rails and snipe distributed nationwide)

Big Game

Black bear (nationwide)
Black-tailed deer (Pacific coast)
Mule deer (west)
White-tailed deer (nationwide)
Elk (west)
Moose (Rockies)
Mountain goat (Rockies)
Bighorn sheep (west of Great Plains)

Varmints

Bobcat (east of Continental Divide)
Coyote (mainly west of Mississippi River)
Crow (nationwide)

Fox (nationwide)
Gopher (Great Plains)
Jackrabbit (west of Mississippi River)
Magpie (west of Mississippi)
Mountain lion (west of Rockies)
Opossum (east and midwest)
Prairie dog (west and southwest)
Raccoon (nationwide)
Woodchuck (east, north-central)

● **Firearms and other weapons.** A gun is not essential to the country dweller. All guns are dangerous. But if you must have one, these are the facts
about them. Air guns: Firing a small lead pellet, the
modern air rifle is a precision weapon weighing
about 8 lb; fitted with telescopic sights, a .22 model
is accurate and powerful enough to be used in
shooting rats, starlings, sparrows and small deer
within a range of up to 70 yd. It makes no noise, so
that if one misses the target one can recock, load
and fire again without disturbing the prey, scoring
a kill perhaps with a second or third shot. Avoid an
air rifle which is cocked by a breaking action: the
barrel and air chamber are best when made in one
piece. Sporting rifles: Of greater power than the air
rifle of the same caliber, lighter in weight, and better suited for killing hares, rabbits, squirrels, etc., is
the miniature .22 rifle firing the long cartridge; but
its great range makes it dangerous, as even with

the short rifle cartridge the bullet may carry nearly 1,000 yd, and it should not be used near any built-up area.

Shotguns: The difference between a shotgun and a rifle is that whereas the rifle has a spirally grooved barrel which imparts a deadly velocity and accuracy to its single lead bullet, a shotgun has a smooth barrel and fires not a bullet but a spreading flight of small lead shot with a maximum killing range of about 50 yd. The most favored is the double-barreled 12-bore shotgun, which gives the user a second chance of bringing down his quarry. These are expensive. Single-barrel shotguns are very much cheaper. The 12-bore is good for all kinds of game. A smaller shotgun, the .410 or "four-ten," is used for pests and vermin, and will shoot rabbits and pigeons at 30 yd: these are cheaper still.

An old gun bought at an auction sale may have been made before black gunpowder had been replaced by modern smokeless nitro powder. If so, it should be "nitro-proved" by a gunsmith before it is used with modern cartridges; failing this, it must be used only with black-powder cartridges, for there is danger that nitro-powder ammunition will burst the gun. The owner of a black-powder gun can load his own cartridges if he has permission to buy and store the powder. Modern cartridge cases will not take the full black-powder charge of 3 drams (in a

12-bore) with 1⅛ oz. of shot. Don't, then, buy a new gun that has not been nitro-proved. Look carefully at an old one.

Of other weapons only two need be considered, the longbow and the crossbow. One does not need mighty muscles to draw the modern bow, which is not the solid yew longbow but resembles rather the composite bow of antiquity which drove its arrow through the power provided by a careful blending of flexible wood, horn and sinew. The modern bow is a laminated structure built up from wafer-thin layers of very strong elastic materials such as fiberglass and specially selected hardwood, the laminations being bonded by synthetic resin adhesives while clamped over a former, the shaping being done as the bow is built up. Solid fiberglass and tubular steel bows are also made, the latter having an excellent cast. Unlike the wooden and to some extent the composite bow, the steel bow is not affected by weather, does not let down during a shoot and so does not call, as does the wooden bow, for a constant raising of the point of aim.

An archer should use the strongest bow he can handle without fatigue in a full day's shoot. While the average healthy man can handle a bow with a draw weight of 40–45 lb., a very strong man might do better with a bow up to 50 lb. When hunting, it is necessary to know the accurate range of one's bow and to keep within it. The accurate range of a bow depends on its weight and the weight and design of the arrow used: the lighter the arrow the further it can fly. Assuming that bow and arrow are properly matched, and beginning with a bow of not less than 35 lb. weight, allow 1 yd. of distance to be shot for each pound pull of the bow, up to 60 yd.—beyond which calculation errs. No archer can be sure of killing large game more than 50 yd. away. Allow only 25 yd. for birds, rabbits and squirrels.

More powerful and deadly than the longbow is the modern hunting crossbow. With its gunlike stock of walnut or mahogany and its laminated alloy or melamine barrel, its bow prod of 42-ton tensile alloy, strung with a Dacron bowstring, and fitted with telescopic sights, it has draw weights ranging from 45 lb. in models for use by women and children to 130 lb. for the hunting of really large game. A draw weight of 130 lb. gives the arrow, or bolt, a range of 400 yd. For all-round shooting, a draw weight of 100 lb. is considered adequate, with a range of 360 yd. All bows are very much simpler and cheaper than guns and of course are quite silent in action.

The traditional 6-ft. longbow can be made by anyone with some skill in carpentry and a vice, a clamp, a block plane, a spokeshave, a drawknife, a couple of files, some garnet paper and steel wool. The best wood is yew, not the quick-growing yew of the local churchyard but the mountain yew found especially in Spain and Portugal. Other woods are wych elm, hazel and ash. With yew, the wood used is mainly that nearest the outside of the log, the light-colored sapwood just beneath the bark. Being resistant to stretch, it makes the bow's back (the convex side when bent) while the belly is made from the darker, compression-resistant heartwood. For beginners, the best wood for a first bow, since it is easy to work, is a South American hardwood called lemonwood. The earliest longbows were made in one piece from a stave about 1½ in. sq., but the problems arising from the difficulty of getting an exactly equal bend from each limb were such as to oblige later bow makers to begin by selecting a short, wide stave which they split from end to end, bringing the two halves together butt to butt and glueing them in a fishtail joint to form one long stave with more or less balanced properties. Whatever wood is used it must be flat-grained; quarter- or off-grained staves make bows that tend to go out of line. The size of the bow is determined by the length of the arrow, and that in turn by the length of your arms. To find the right length of arrow for yourself, take a broomstick in your left hand and hold it at arm's length parallel to your left side. Standing erect and at right angles to the left arm, turn your head left and focus your eyes on the first joint of your left hand. With assistance, measure the distance from that joint to your right eye. Subtract 1½ in. from the result. This will be your own arrow length.

To find the corresponding length for the bow, take as standard the 6-ft. bow and the 28-in. arrow. For every inch or fraction of an inch subtracted from the length of the standard arrow in your own case, subtract twice that amount from the length of the bow. No arrow should exceed 28 in. Bowstrings are made from nonstretch waxed linen thread. A cable-type fishing line with a known breaking strain may be used; enough threads should be taken into the string to add up to 200 lb. (or 150 lb. for a 30-lb. bow), so that if a line with a 10-lb. breaking strain is used, you will need twenty lines. Arrows may be made from straight birch dowel rods of 5/16-in. diameter. Instructions for making such bows and arrows are to be found in several books, including *Archery Handbook* by Edmund H. Burke (1976).

For rabbit shooting, target arrows are used; for shooting gray squirrels, crows, and tree pests, arrows fitted with a hardwood knob are preferred; these will stun or kill small game at close range but will bounce off if they hit the tree. Arrowheads are normally of steel, but it is remarkable that flint arrowheads are superior to metal ones, the natural conchoidal fracture of flint giving the head about 25 percent more penetration power. Glass, too, from broken bottles, has an extremely sharp cutting edge.

Worthy of mention as a hunting weapon is the now obsolescent throw stick of the country laborer, carried in the coat pocket and used for knocking out small game at a distance of 30 yd. The short stick or cudgel is thickened and weighted at one end, this being the end held when the stick is thrown. It revolves in the air and the clubbed end strikes the quarry. In expert hands it is a deadly weapon, hitting its target with great force.

A. EDIBLE ANIMALS

● **Rabbits and hares.** The cottontail, the most common of American rabbit species, is also the most abundant of game animals. Millions of cottontails are shot every year. These herbivorous animals are renowned for their formidable powers of propagation. They breed mainly between February and August but sometimes through October in the Gulf states. They become sexually active at 5 months and have a gestation period of 29–30 days. The does produce three or four litters a year, with three to six young in each litter. Given maximum fertility, maximum food supply and freedom from predators, it has been calculated that one mother could give rise to over a million descendants in 4 years! A rabbit consumes its own weight in bark, roots, grain and greens many times over each week and is thus a major competitor for human food supplies. Wild rabbits weigh about 3 lb., tame ones double that figure.

Hares. (jackrabbits, snowshoes rabbits) belong to the same genus as rabbits but usually are larger and have darker fur. They are longer-legged and often have black-tipped ears. They do not burrow nor are they gregarious like rabbits, but produce their young—with eyes open and complete with fur—aboveground. They lie singly in their form in the fields, and when startled, career in huge leaps, propelled by their kangaroolike back legs. Their speed protects them from enemies. Both rabbits and hares are edible, the flesh of the rabbit being white and tender, that of the hare coarser, redder and more gamy. Hare is messier to prepare for the pot.

Traps. Shooting apart, both rabbits and hares may be taken in traps, of which the most used is the looped-wire snare. Ready-made snares may be bought for a few dollars in country towns, but they can be as well made at home. One trap can be made from 6 ft. of brass wire of the correct gauge, folded into four with its strands twisted into a single cable. Do this by fixing one end of a galvanized steel S hook to a heavyish weight and pushing the other through the two loops formed by the doubling of the strands of wire. Hold one end of the wire, let the weight hang down and set it spinning rapidly, having first set a small brass eyelet in the double loop. Now thread the upper end of the cable through the eyelet. Take the upper end, bend back about an inch of it and twist it around the strands to form a ¼-in. loop. Next take a 3-ft. length of strong string, double it and put the doubled end through the small end loop on the wire. Slip the two loose ends through the looped end, like a slipknot, and pull tight. Now knot the free ends of the string around a wooden peg about 1 ft. long, notched at the top to receive the string and pointed at the other end for driving into the ground. This completes the snare. Only one more thing is to be done: if the loop runs all the way it will tighten cruelly round the neck of the rabbit which runs its head into it and slowly strangle it. To prevent this, knot the wire 6 in. from the brass eyelet so that it will not pass through it: the noose cannot then be tightened beyond that point. The snared rabbit will either break its neck or will wait quietly in the snare until released and despatched. Before using a new snare, hang it up to weather for a day or two.

To set a snare, find the rabbit's habitual run. Choose a point halfway between two of its sets of footprints (rabbits are leapers) and knock the peg into the ground about a foot to one side of the run. Rub your hands on the ground to get rid of the human smell, to which rabbits are sensitive, and open the noose to about 4 in. across. Find a pointed stick about 6 in. long, sharpen one end to a point and make a groove in the other end to support the noose. Press the wire near the noose into the groove in the stick, and push the pointed end into the ground. The noose should now stand upright across the run, its lower edge being a handsbreadth high for rabbits, for hares half a hand higher. Visit the snare first thing in the morning and last thing at night.

In *The Gamekeeper at Home* (1878), Richard Jefferies stresses that practice and skill are essential to the successful snaring of hares. The loop of the snare must be neither too large nor too small, it must be set at the right height above the ground, which is "measured by placing the clenched fist on the earth and then putting the extended thumb of the other open hand upon it, stretching it out as in the action of spanning, when the tip of the little finger gives the right height for the lower bend of the loop— that is, as a rule. . . . A hare carries his head much higher than might be thought; and he is very strong, so that the plug which holds the wire must be driven in firmly to withstand his first convulsive struggle. The small upright stick whose cleft suspends the wire across the 'run' must not be put too near the hare's path, or he will see it, and it must be tolerably stiff, or his head will push the wire aside." However, some people believe that it is wrong to drive the holding peg too firmly into the ground, because a hare caught in anything firm will scream, whereas if it is caught in something that moves, it will go on jumping about in an effort to get free and so will quickly tire itself out and lie still. But clearly the peg must not be so loose that it is pulled out of the ground and the hare allowed to run away with it.

Jefferies further describes how hares may be caught with no aid but the hand, especially in winter weather when the cold makes all wild animals "dummel," or slow to move. "It requires a practiced eye, that knows precisely where to look among the grass, to detect him hidden in the bunch under the dead, dry bennets. An inexperienced person chancing to see a hare sitting like this would naturally stop short in walking to get a better view; whereupon the animal, feeling that he was observed, would instantly make a rush. You must persuade the hare that he is unseen; and so long as he notices no start or sign of recognition—his eye is on you from first entering the field—he will remain still, believing that you will pass.

"The poacher, having marked his game, looks steadily in front of him, never turning his head, but insensibly changes his course and quietly approaches him sidelong. Then, in the moment of passing, he falls quick as lightning on his knee, and seizes the hare just behind the (head). It is the only place where the sudden grasp would hold him in his convulsive terror . . . and almost ere he can shriek (as he will do) the left hand has tightened round the hind legs. Stretching him to his full length across the knee, the right thumb, with a peculiar twist, dislocates his neck, and he is dead in an instant. . . . It is very easy to sprain the thumb while learning the trick.

"A poacher will sometimes place his hat gently on the ground, when first catching sight of a sitting hare, and then stealthily approach on the opposite side. The hare watches the hat, while the real enemy comes up unawares, or, if both are seen, he is in doubt which way to dash."

In the absence of a snare, make a deadfall trap by propping up a stone slab with a baited twig, to reach which the victim must reach up and, moving the twig, cause the slab to fall and crush it. Another trap is the figure-four trap, in which the three wooden supports used form a 4. First, a sharpened base support is stuck vertically into the ground; then a crosspiece is notched in the center to fit a smaller notch in the center of the upright base support; next the lower end of a slanting lateral spar is fitted into a notch in the end of the crosspiece, its center resting on top of the base piece. This frame is kept in position by the weight of a stone slab leaning against the lateral spar. A bait is placed on the crosspiece, and when this is snatched the edifice collapses on the animal.

Killing rabbits and hares. Rabbits are despatched either by a sharp blow behind the ears or by dislocating the neck by pulling. In the latter case, hold the rabbit's hind legs in the right hand, letting it hang head downwards, then grasp the head with the left hand, fingers under the chin and the thumb extended behind the ears. Stretch the rabbit firmly but without force and then press the chin up and the base of the head down. The force needed varies with the size and age of the animal; it must be enough to dislocate the neck at once without pulling away the head.

To kill by a blow, hold the rabbit by the hind legs. In hanging down, it will normally raise its head, which makes it easy to kill with a karate chop at the back of the neck.

Paunching. When killed, the rabbit or hare should have its hind legs slit just above each hock between the sinew and the bone so that a skewer or cord can be passed through, enabling it to be hung up for the blood to drain into the neck. Before it can be skinned it must be paunched. Having covered the kitchen table with newspaper, lay the animal on its back with its head away from you and slit open the belly with scissors or a sharp knife. First cut through the pelt, laying it carefully aside, then make a shallow cut in the inner skin. Take out the intestines, wrap in newspaper and discard, saving only the heart, liver and kidneys. Wipe with a damp clean cloth. After paunching, skin and cook a rabbit as soon as possible, but hang a hare 3–6 days according to the weather.

To skin a rabbit, first cut the skin round the lower joint of the hind legs, completely severing the paws. Push the hind legs up to the belly, holding tight to the pelt, which will pull away without trouble. Ease the pelt over the rump, cutting off the tail if necessary. Sever the front paws at the lower joint and pull the front legs through the pelt. Cut off the head with the pelt complete. A rabbit is trussed for cooking by laying it on its back, bringing the back legs inwards to the middle of the belly and fastening them with string, the front legs being treated in the same way.

● **Squirrels.** The native gray squirrel eats not only woodland foods but cultivated nuts, garden fruits and the eggs and young of birds. It lives in nests, or "dreys," in trees, sometimes in tree holes and sometimes in old nests of magpies and crows. It has two broods a year, each with about five young. Its flesh is edible and resembles rabbit in flavor. Paunch, skin and truss as for the rabbit, and use within 3 days. Cook as rabbit.

● **Venison** is the culinary term for the flesh of deer of all kinds and is sometimes extended to include goat flesh, which is similar. The flesh of the forest-fed animal is considered the choicest, but since venison improves with age, an old animal is preferred to a young one. Skin as soon as shot. The meat is improved by moderate hanging—not more than 2 weeks in a cool, dry place. Only the haunch and saddle are worth roasting, the rest being stewed or made into pies. When hung the meat must be examined each day for signs of tainting by running a small knife into it; if when withdrawn the blade has an unpleasant smell, the tainted parts must be washed with warm milk and water, dried and covered with ground ginger and pepper— which must be removed before cooking. The haunch is cooked by rubbing it all over with fat and covering it with greased paper over which is then brushed a paste of flour and water, this being covered with more greased paper tied in place with string, the whole then being roasted before a glowing fire or in a moderate oven for 3–4 hours, with frequent basting. Half an hour before serving, the paper and paste are removed, the joint dredged lightly with flour and basted with hot butter until it has a good brown color.

● **Woodchuck.** This animal, also known as the groundhog, is terrestrial and active during the day. It eats green vegetation and is found throughout the Northeast. It nests and hibernates in burrows (whence, according to legend, it emerges on February 2 and, if it sees its shadow, returns for 6 more weeks of winter). Its flesh is mild in flavor. Paunch and, if caught just before hibernation, remove the insulating layer of fat. Cut into pieces and parboil in salted water 1 hour. Roll in flour and fry in hot fat until brown.

● **Raccoon.** This nocturnal mammal is found virtually everywhere in North America in wooded areas. It feeds along streams and lakes and is highly omnivorous. To fricassee, first clean, remove fat, parboil and cut into pieces. Dip in flour salted and peppered to taste, brown in hot fat and simmer for 2 hours in 2 cups broth.

B. EDIBLE BIRDS

The usual way of obtaining birds for the table is to shoot them. They may also be taken by means of netting, cages, birdlime or inebriants, or by using falcons or hawks. The last, being a recondite form of sport, need not concern us. The others are illegal except for purposes of scientific study.

The netting of birds is usually carried out at night, all that is needed being some lengths of fish netting draped between trees or on poles and a flashlight. The light is shone on the net and the awakened birds dash towards it and become entangled in the mesh, from which they are removed and killed. Cage traps for birds are made of wire netting on wood frames and work on the principle that access is made easier than egress. Such a trap, baited with grain, is left in some place frequented by the kind of bird one is after. It must have room enough for a good number of birds and a small door through which trapped birds can be withdrawn. Keepers use such traps to obtain game birds for breeding at the end of the season. Liming is an ancient way of catching birds by spreading birdlime on the ground, on the twigs of trees or on wire netting. The use of inebriants involves soaking a quantity of wheat, rye, barley or peas in a narcotic liquor, strewing them on the land where the birds are to be taken and picking up the befuddled or insensible birds before their systems have recovered from the intoxication. A game book of 1686 recommends soaking the grain in an infusion of nux-vomica, a seed containing strychnine; in the lees of wine; or in the juice of hemlock mixed with the seeds of henbane and poppy. Poachers have long known this trick but usually soak the grain in rum or whisky. The dregs of the must of a homemade wheat wine have been found equally effective. A way of trapping pheasants in winter is to ram a large bottle neck downwards in hard snow and withdraw it, leaving a firm impression of the bottle. If the narrow part of the impression is filled with dried peas soaked in water, a pheasant, in taking the peas, will lean further and further over until it topples with its head in the hole.

Game birds are killed by pressing the crossed thumbs down on the back of the skull. This is less easy the older and larger the bird. The old fowler's method is to bite the skull between the teeth. Alternatively, hold the bird by the body and sharply rap the back of the skull and neck over the toe or heel of your boot.

● **Preparing poultry and game.** These instructions apply to domestic poultry as well as to game. To pluck a bird while still warm—if it has gone cold, dip it into hot water for 1 minute—suspend it, if heavy, from a hook, or hold it in the left hand if light, and pull out the wing feathers first, then continue across the back and breast. To singe, wrap the bird in a sheet of dry newspaper, place on a metal grid and ignite the paper. Or hold the bird's neck in one hand and with the other apply the flame from a twist of lighted paper. To draw, cut off the head and neck, remove windpipe and crop, cutting the skin attaching the crop to the carcass. Sever legs 2 in. below joint, bend and break them off, then pull out the tendons one at a time, having wound the ends around a skewer. Cut the skin between vent and tail and with two fingers inserted loosen the bird's innards from the stomach walls, being careful not to break the gall bladder. Gently pull out the whole innards. Wash the bird under running cold water and dry with a cloth. Wash liver and heart in cold water. To disjoint, cut the skin around the thigh, then cut through the joint and remove leg and thigh. Cut through base of wing and remove by cutting it away from the breast at the joint. Remove the other leg and wing and split the bird in two with a knife, separating breast from back and ribs. To truss, place bird on its breast and cross the ends of the wings over the back of its neck. Hold the legs and, pressing the thighs into the sides of the bird, pass a needle and thread through the bottom of one thigh, through the body and out through the other thigh. Turn bird on its breast and pass needle through the middle of pinion, fastening with it the skin to the back and bringing the string out through the other pinion. Pull ends of string tight and tie together at the side. Turn bird on its back, pass the needle and thread through the skin, over the bottom of the breastbone, over one leg and through back of bird, and tie it over the legs at the other side.

Some birds are too small to pluck, in which case they are skinned by slitting the skin down the back and gently working it away from the bird, complete with feathers. To make this easier, the wings, and the feet from the knee joint, are first removed.

Crow.   Parboil dressed bird and then roast, broil or stew.

Dove.   Draw the dove, which should be a young one, as soon as killed and cook within 4 days.

Pluck, singe and clean, wash well and dry. Cut off the head close to body, saving the neck to make gravy, and sever feet at first joint. With a needle run a fine string through both legs and body, bring the string up round the rump and tie the legs up to it. Broil, braise, fry, grill, stew or put into a pie.

Duck. Truss for roasting. Place in a deep baking pan with ½ in. boiling salted water in the bottom and bake for 10 minutes to remove fishy taint. Dry the bird, dredge with flour, baste with butter and roast in front of the fire for 20 minutes; or bake for 20 minutes in a moderate oven, basting frequently.

Goose. Hang for 10 days or so, singe, clean and dry. Rub inside with salt and pepper, sew up and brush with oil. Sear over a hot fire or in a very hot oven, then cook for 1½–2 hours at a low, constant heat.

Grouse. Halve and rub with melted butter or oil, sear quickly over high heat and then cook slowly until done. Turn occasionally, basting frequently with a mixture of melted butter, lemon juice, pepper and salt.

Partridge. Hang for not more than 4 days. Stuff with vine leaves sprinkled with brandy; roast as pheasant; remove and discard vine leaves. Old birds should be casseroled.

Pheasant. Hang for up to 3 weeks. The hen is preferred. To roast, first pluck, clean and draw, keeping tail feathers for garnish. Put 2 oz. butter and a shallot inside the bird, wrap two rashers bacon around the breast. Cover with greaseproof paper and roast for up to 1 hour, according to size. Dredge with flour, baste and return to oven to brown. Garnish with watercress and serve with bread sauce.

Quail. Halve, dip in milk, roll in flour-salt-pepper mixture and brush lightly with beaten egg yolk. Drop one or two pieces at a time into hot, deep fat. When birds are a rich brown, remove from fat and drain.

Snipe. The weight of this small game bird varies from 2–10 oz. Roast for a few minutes on a spit over charcoal without cleaning the bird. Or place on a slice of buttered toast in a roasting pan and roast for 15–20 minutes. Serve with lemon and melted butter on toast.

Woodcock. The male bird is preferred. Hang for 2–8 days until mature. Pluck the body, skin the head and neck. Do not draw. For roasting, truss, brush with melted butter and cook as snipe.

C. EGGS, FROGS AND SNAILS

The eggs of most birds are edible, but wild birds' eggs are often too small and too bitter in taste to be worth gathering, while most people today feel some compunction about taking eggs, which is in any case now illegal, with some exceptions.

That snails and frogs are edible is well known. Henry Mayhew in *London Labour and the London Poor* records a conversation he had circa 1850 with a young street seller of birds' nests and wild foods who sold snails and frogs to Frenchmen. The Frenchmen, it appears, always picked out first the yellow-bellied frogs—"the others they're afraid is toads." Of snails:

"The snails I sell by the pailful—at 2s. 6d. the pail. There is some hundreds in a pail. The wet weather is the best times for catching 'em; the French people eats 'em. They boils 'em first to get 'em out of the shell and get rid of the green froth; then they boils them again, and after that in vinegar. They eats 'em hot, but some of the foreigners like 'em cold. They say they're better, if possible, than whelks."

Had Mayhew been an American, the two kinds of frogs mentioned might well have been the leopard frog and the green frog, two very common species. For table purposes, however, the most important species is the giant bullfrog. Frogs are caught in ponds and slow streams by means of nets and a wooden rake or by spearing. It is the hind legs which are eaten. Cooking is simple, the frogs' legs being floured, seasoned and lightly fried in a little butter for 10–12 minutes, or dipped in melted, seasoned butter and grilled for 5 minutes.

Common garden snails also make perfectly good eating. If collected wild, they should be starved for 2 days (or until they stop foaming) before using. Cook by throwing them into a pot of boiling water for 20 minutes. Remove from shells, take out the small intestine, then cook in a saucepan with butter, flour, stock and various seasonings.

D. FRESHWATER FISHES

The United States has a remarkable network of lakes and rivers, most of them fish-bearing except where the pollutions of industry have killed off the fish. There are also innumerable streams and brooks, canals, reservoirs, gravel and clay pits, all of which may contain edible fish, sometimes of large size. Of river fish, the salmon and the trout, which belong to the same family, are the most prized both for sport and for eating. They are jealously preserved and are caught with a fly mainly by skilled anglers. Most other fish are caught with submerged baits by unprivileged but no less devoted anglers who often do not sell or eat their catch but weigh and measure it and throw it back into the water. While not such delicate eating as fish of the salmon family, other fish are nevertheless edible. Some of them have an insipid or "muddy" flavor; the latter may be removed by keeping the fish alive in a tank of clear water for a few days before it is eaten. Most fish taste well when newly caught if gutted, wiped and lightly grilled over charcoal, with a little butter and some herbs. Some fish attain a remarkable size if left in peace to grow, for the life-span of fishes like the pike and carp may exceed that of a man. Pike have been caught weighing over 46 lb., carp over 55 lb., and largemouth bass more than 22 lb. A brown trout long on the records list was close to 40 lb., while a chinook salmon will grow up to 100 lb.

Nor is there a necessary relation between the size of a stream and the size of the fish to be found in it, for since the smallest stream connects with a larger one, and that eventually to the broad river which runs to the sea, a large fish may find its way upstream to a small brook. A stream near your homestead small enough for you to jump across may contain a variety of fish, especially if it has some deep pools and clean, aerated water. And among the fish may be the occasional one of large size.

As with game, there are closed and open seasons and catch limits for many fish. Again, these vary widely from place to place. There are some bodies of water in the United States which have year-round seasons and no catch limits. Consult your state department of conservation for particulars.

There is a broad distinction between those fish which live in deep, slow-flowing water with weedy stretches, deep pools, bends and canal-like sections (i.e., bass, carp, perch, crappie, drum, catfish and walleye) and those which prefer fast shallows and middling deep reaches of medium flow (i.e., muskie, shad and whitefish). Table IV is intended as a rough guide to the most common freshwater fish. It describes them in broad terms, taking little note of the various species and regional differentiations, and gives the weight of the average catch. Individual specimens may vary considerably from these norms.

The baits used by anglers are varied, ranging from items in or near to the fishes' natural diet at the one end to macaroni, sausage and cheese at the other. Some anglers employ "dopes" and flavorings like oil of fennel and aniseed oil to attract fish. The standard ground bait for getting fish to feed is ground-up stale bread. But there are other ways of taking fish than by angling, sometimes illegal, sometimes not. For example:

Fish trap. A willow or wicker framework covered with net, and with a retracted mouth which gradually narrows in the manner of a lobster pot, making it easier for a fish to enter than get out, is placed at a strategic point in the stream and inspected from

time to time for captive fish. Portable fish traps of
wire mesh, 3 ft. and 4 ft. long, of a barrel shape,
with funnels from each end, are supplied by Orvis
of Boston, Inc. 213 West Plain St. Wayland, Mass.
01778. They are baited with worms, offal or herring
guts tied in muslin or put in a punched tin. Other
traps are made with straight sides, and there are
models for catching different fish, including eels
and pike.

Trot lines. Baited lines are left out overnight attached to pegs in the bank, and the catch drawn in
in the morning. Or lines are tied to overhanging
branches so that the wind moves the trailing fly or
bait in an attractive way on the stream. Or a line is
tied to two stones, with several baited hooks attached on auxiliary lines; dropped into a stream, its
position is marked and the line retrieved later with
a hooked stick.

Hunting with gaff or spear. Eels are hunted with a
special barbed, three-pronged eel spear called a
pritch. Other large fish are sometimes speared or
gaffed after being attracted to the surface by a light.

Tickling trout. Having made out the position of a
fish and lying down on the bank above it, the
hunter slowly slips his bare arm into the water with
his hand as close as possible to the fish. Passing his
fingers under the belly, he gently rubs it. The fish

Table IV FRESHWATER FISH

Fish	Description	Habitat & Range	Food	Bait	Size	Edibility
Bass	black to dark green back, green to green-brown sides, often with horizontal band from head to tail	weedy lakes, rivers, backwaters nationwide	insects, minnows, small animals, crustaceans	minnows, night crawlers, frogs, surface lures	3-10 lb	good
black crappie	olive-green back, silvery olive sides, irregular dark splotches, spiny dorsal fin	cool, clear, weedy lakes and rivers, northern U.S.	plankton, worms, baitfish	minnows, grubs, dragonflies, crickets	1-2 lb	fair
bluegill	color varies from yellow-orange to dark blue, with irregular vertical bars on sides and long, pointed fins	quiet, weedy lakes or streams nationwide	plankton, plants, insects	dry flies, most other baits	1-3 lb	fair
carp	long and sleek with large scales, barbels at mouth corners, olive to brown back, golden-yellow sides	shallow weedy lakes, quiet reaches of slow rivers nationwide	plants, insects	lugworms, cornmeal, potatoes, doughballs	8-15 lb	good

cat-fish	steely blue back shading to white on belly, forked tail, eight barbels on mouth	lakes, large rivers in most of U.S.	bottom feeder	worms, night crawlers, crayfish, doughballs	2–10 lb	fair
cisco	bluish to greenish back, silvery body; resembles whitefish	cold, clear, deep lakes from the Great Lakes east	bottom-dwelling insects	dry flies	vari-able, 7 lb maximum	good
drum	pearl-gray back, silvery sides, blunt head, rounded tail, humped back	large lakes and large slow rivers from Atl. coast to Mo. River drainage	mollusks, crayfish	crayfish, baitfish	1–5 lb	fair
eel	snakelike body fringed with fins	crevices in river and lake bottoms east of Rockies	frogs, newts, spawn, fry	small dead fish, worms	5 lb	good
muskie	green to brown to gray usually with vertical bars; scaleless on lower cheek and gill covers	clear rivers, lakes and streams in eastern and north-central U.S.	fish, animals, birds, snakes	mice, baitfish	10–20 lb	very good
salmon	blue-green-gray back, silver-white belly; often black-spotted	fast-running rocky and sandy streams, Northeast and Pacific Northwest; deep, cold Maine lakes (landlocked)	minnows, worms, flies, trout fry	worms, dry flies	5–20 lb	highly esteemed

	Appearance	Habitat	Food	Bait	Weight	Rating
shad	greenish back, silvery body	Atlantic and Pacific coastal rivers and streams	plankton	dry flies, lures, no live bait	3–6 lb	good
trout	olive green to dark blue back, black-and red-spotted back and sides, forked tail	fast-running streams and gravel beds in most of U.S.	crustaceans,	worms, dry flies,	1–4 lb	highly esteemed
wall-eye	oblong olive-gray body, large opaque eyes	deep, slow-flowing waters in East and most of far West and South	crayfish, frogs, small fishes	live and dead bait	1–4 lb	very good
white crap-pie	similar to black crappie, but with seven to nine dark vertical bands	silty rivers and lakes, bayous, southern U.S.	plankton, worms, baitfish	minnows, grubs, dragonflies, crickets	1–2 lb	fair
white-fish	brown to olive back, silvery sides, large dorsal fin, elongated body with conical head	cold, swift streams and clear, deep lakes, northern U.S.	insects, larvae, spawn	dry flies, live bait, lures	1–3 lb	good
yellow perch	olive back, golden-yellow sides, elongated hump-backed body, spiny dorsal fin, barred markings	still waters and ponds, most of U.S.	insects, worms, small fish	worms, live bait	1–2 lb	very good

Carp · · · · · · · Crayfish

Perch

Trout

Fig. 15

will slowly rise, enabling the hand to position itself
for the decisive grab; finger and thumb inserted
into the gills and the fish suddenly jerked up and
out.

● **Snaring large fish with wire loop.** Richard
Jefferies (op. cit.) describes how jacks were taken
with a long slender ash stick to which was attached
a loop and running noose of thin copper wire. Acting as quietly and invisibly as possible, the hunter,
having marked his prey in the shallow, would extend the rod across the water 3 or 4 yd. upstream,
letting it swim down with the current until it
reached the fish, when it was slipped over its head
past jaws, gills and first fins until it came to a place
about one third of the way down the fish's length,
when the hunter cleared his arm and, with a sudden jerk, lifted the fish right out of the stream on to
the bank. The effect of this was to momentarily
paralyze the fish, sometimes to kill it. Lacking a
wire, says Jefferies, the skillful hunter would make
do with a peeled and twisted withe, a noose and
running knot being made in the stick itself—but
this required rather greater dexterity than the wire.

Netting fish. Jefferies also describes how a net
would be stretched from bank to bank and watched
by one man while his fellow walked up the brook
30 or 40 yd. and drove the fish down the current
towards it by thrashing the water with a pole.

When the cork floats bobbed under water, the watcher knew that a shoal of fish had run into it, drew the string and made his haul.

Other methods. A sledgehammer brought down hard on a rock in a shallow stream will set up shock waves in the water, stunning any nearby fish, which can then be netted or picked up by hand. A temporary dam built above a pool will sometimes sufficiently empty the pool of water for any trout it contains to be caught by hand.

A way of taking trout from a small brook so overgrown with briars and thorn that it is impossible to use a rod and line is to lower a worm on some heavily weighted extrastrong tackle threaded through an old brass curtain rod. The bait is pulled up to the end of the tube, the tube pushed through the bushes, and the bait taken to the water by the weight. When hooked, the fish is pulled in until it is struggling at the end of the rod. The fisherman then simply walks backward and hauls in the catch.

The refraction of light in water, which makes it difficult to gauge the true position of a fish, can be obviated by the wearing of polaroid glasses. Through these, fish can be seen which are invisible to the naked eye.

● Cooking

Bass. Draw, fillet and marinate in 3 tbsp. seasoned oil for 15 minutes. Broil fillets approximately 5 minutes without turning, basting twice. Or broil the whole dressed fish 5–6 minutes on each side, season and serve with melted butter.

Bluegill. Remove heads, tails, fins and innards, leaving skin. Split down center. Brush with a mixture of lemon juice, parsley, salt and pepper. Place on grill, skin side towards heat source, broil 5 minutes, brush with herb mixture and broil 5 minutes more. Pour remaining sauce over fish, garnish with lemon wedges and serve.

Carp. Soak well in running water, then in weak vinegar and salted water. May be baked, roasted, broiled, fried, stewed or cooked in wine.

Catfish. Keep alive until ready to eat. Then, starting on underside, cut head almost off, grip it and remove skin. (Watch out for the "whiskers," or barbels, which can cause painful wounds.) Roll catfish in a mixture of half flour, half yellow cornmeal, salted and peppered to taste. Fry in hot bacon grease until golden brown, turning once (about 4 minutes per side).

Cisco. As for whitefish.

Crappie.   Draw and wipe with damp cloth. Fry in melted butter over medium flame about 3 minutes on one side, 5 minutes on the other. Lower flame and sprinkle with paprika, salt and pepper to taste. Garnish with watercress and serve. Or prepare as catfish.

Drum.   As for carp.

Eel.   Eels are killed with a knife thrust through the base of the skull or by knocking their heads hard on a stone. Skin an eel by holding its head, covered with a cloth, in one hand and cutting around the neck with the other. Turn the skin down an inch, grip it and strip it off. Chop off head and tail of the skinned eel, open the throat with a knife point and make a cut at the navel; then push the gut with a skewer from the small hole in the navel through the opening at the throat. Wash and dry before cooking. Eels may be made into pies or soup, or boiled, fried or stewed. To make eel pie, cut the skinned eel into pieces, season with pepper and salt and place in a greased pie dish. Cover with milk and water and a flaky pastry crust and bake until brown.

Muskie.   As for catfish or salmon.

Salmon.   Season several 1-in.-thick slices with salt, pepper and lemon juice. Place in a buttered dish and bake in a moderate oven 20–30 minutes. If you wish, add some chopped vegetables (onions, tomatoes, mushrooms, celery).

Shad. Scale, draw and remove fins. Score crosswise several times on each side. Salt and pepper the fish inside and out, baste with oil, and let stand for a few minutes. Broil 20 minutes on a plank or broiler plate. Pour 2–3 tbsp. melted butter, lemon juice, salt and pepper over fish and serve.

Trout. Clean and cook soon after catching. To bake, put the whole cleaned fish in a shallow tin or dish, cover with greased paper, bake in a hot oven and serve at once. To broil, split the trout down the back, season with salt, pepper and lemon juice and rub with oil. Cook under a red-hot grill or over charcoal for 5–10 minutes. To fry, split fish and remove the bones, dip in beaten egg and breadcrumbs and fry in hot fat. Garnish with fried parsley.

Walleye. Prepare as for catfish or follow the method for roasting pike recommended by Isaac Walton in *The Compleat Angler*. Run a spit through the mouth and out the tail, and tie six split sticks lengthwise along the body to prevent the flesh from falling off while cooking. Then "let him be roasted very leisurely, and often basted with claret wine and anchovies and butter mixed together, and also

with what moisture falls from him into the pan."
Don't try this method unless your walleye is a particularly large specimen.

Whitefish. Scale, draw, fillet and wipe dry.
Brush with oil and broil 10–12 minutes on flesh side
and 5–6 minutes on skin side. Season with salt,
pepper and melted butter and garnish with lemon
wedges. If possible, broil over hardwood coals.

Minnows. These despised small fishes may be
easily caught in quantity and cooked like whitebait,
a European delicacy. That is, they are tossed whole
into a floured cloth and then emptied into the frying basket of a deep pan, where they are cooked
rapidly until crisp. Serve with lemon juice. Izaac
Walton says of them: ". . . in the spring they make
of them excellent minnow-tansies; for being washed
well in salt, and their heads and tails cut off, and
their guts taken out, and not washed after, they
prove excellent for that use; that is, being fried with
yolks of eggs, the flowers of cowslips, and of prim-
roses, and a little tansy: thus used, they make a
dainty dish of meat."

The crayfish is a freshwater crustacean that looks
like a lobster in miniature. Most American crayfish
are less than 6 in. long, but the European variety is
a good deal larger and is recognized in France as a
gastronomical delicacy. Crayfish make burrows by

the sides of fast-flowing streams and hide under large stones in the riverbed, emerging at night to feed. They can be caught by wading upstream with a net, overturning any large stones, and when one is found, prodding it with a stick, whereupon it will dart backward—into the net; or by finding their holes and pulling them out. Or they can be trapped in wire baskets baited with bacon or fish or meat offal. Prepare by washing well, removing intestinal tract from under the tail with a knife point, and then boiling for 10 minutes in salted water. From this point, several recipes come into play, one of which follows.

For Crayfish Cardinal, made with 15–20 crayfish, melt 4 oz. butter in a saucepan over a low heat, add crayfish, 2 teaspoons chopped chives and 2 tablespoons cognac. Gently mix, and then pour hot Hollandaise sauce over it, continuing to stir. Serve hot.

□ 22 □

EDIBLE WILD PLANTS

Throughout summer and autumn the countryside
of the United States produces a variety of edible
vegetation. The wild vegetable larder is sparse in
concentrated starches and proteins, though fairly
plentiful in greens and salads. Nuts and fruits are
to be found in the autumn; there are a few edible
roots. In winter there is almost nothing. Yet nature
does provide a number of edible substances which
only require finding and gathering to give materials
for salads, soups and stews, flavorings, jams and
wines, "teas" and "coffees," as well as fodder for
beasts.

● **Nuts.**   The nuts of the hazel are found on road-
side bushes and low trees in woods and copses
after the first frost. They should be spread out on

paper or sacking in the sun for a day or two, when the dry husks can be removed and the nuts packed in sealed containers. The American chestnut is threatened with extinction by chestnut blight, but it is still possible in some areas to find healthy trees and collect their nuts. Stripped from husks, they are spread out to dry and packed in sand or sawdust. They may be boiled, roasted or ground into a flour for making a kind of bread. Beechnuts, or mast, are sweet in taste but contain traces of a poisonous narcotic called fagin, which disappears after drying. They may also be ground into flour. Walnuts, butternuts and hickory nuts are common in many parts of the country and make good eating.

Acorns are collected in the fall, skinned, chopped small, oven-dried and stored in tight containers; they may be ground into a flour as required. Alternatively, crack their shells, soak for 24 hours, changing the water frequently. Remove shells and boil the kernels, changing water every 2 hours until the bitter taste has gone. Dry and use as flour.

Oil from nuts.   A very sweet olivelike oil may be expressed from beechnuts, and a bland, fixed oil from hazelnuts, as well as from the cultivated walnut.

Nuts as fodder.   After the extraction of oil the res-

Marsh Mallow   Dandelion   Bitter Vetch

Wild Parsnip   Flowering Rush

Fig. 16

idue of the nuts may be mixed with other foods and fed to cattle. Acorns make fodder for pigs, as does beech mast: the whole acorn may be coarsely ground, the meal then being boiled or scalded and mixed with cattle beet or other fodder. The horse chestnut, unfit for humans, may be fed to cattle, sheep and poultry after first removing the bitter taste by soaking the partly crushed nuts in cold water for 8 hours, boiling for 30 minutes, grinding or crushing to a meal and mixing with other meals in the proportion of about 40 to 60.

● **Roots.** Throughout the year the arrowhead may be dug up when found in any quantity in dry woods and grassland. The roots are wholesome and nutritious. Children eat them raw, but they are delicious roasted or boiled, and may be used in soups. Other edible roots which may be boiled and mashed are those of the wild parsnip, the dandelion, the yellow water lily, the marshmallow, the bitter vetch, the silverweed, the Flowering Rush and the wild Jerusalem artichoke.

● **Fruits and berries.** Crab apples—inedible except as jelly. Sloes are the fruit of the blackthorn; they are inedible but make good wine. Wild plums grow on small trees larger and less thorny than the blackthorn; unlike sloes they can be eaten in pies

Charlock   Red Dead-nettle

Fig. 17

and tarts: pick after first frost. Blackberries, in conjunction with apples, make pies, tarts and jam. Elderberries are barely edible on their own but make good wine. The rose hip is made into a vitamin C-rich syrup or a wine. The rowan or mountain ash has berries which may be made into jellies or wine. The bush cranberry is used for tarts and sauces. The cloudberry may be used in several ways. Also edible are: the dewberry, loganberry, salmonberry and hawthorn berries which in spite of their insipid taste can be made into jellies and wine with plenty of sugar. The wild varieties of cherry, currant, raspberry, and strawberry, are also worth gathering.

Leaves and stems. The following are edible in fresh salads: beech leaves, speedwell, cat's-ear, chicory, chickweed, corn salad, thistles, dandelion leaves, wild garlic, black mustard, goatsbeard, miner's lettuce, hairy bittercress, fireweed (willow herb) leaves (treat young shoots as asparagus), hawkbit, burnet, purslane, watercress, wood sorrel (blossoms), yarrow, plantain, lamb's-quarters. Avoid watercress gathered just downstream of a meadow grazed by sheep, as there will be danger of liver fluke.

These (along with many of the above) may be cooked as greens: bistort, charlock, brake (young only), mountain sorrel, good King Henry, goose grass, henbit, cow parsnip, pigweed, red dead nettle, white dead nettle, stinging nettle, sow thistle, shepherd's purse, poke. In general these leaves are cooked like spinach. They are picked when young and tender (with nettles only the tips are used), washed and cooked gently in a saucepan without more water but with a wedge of butter and some seasoning. They may also be made into soups.

These plants have edible stems: burdock, sow thistle, milkweed (also pods), fireweed, horsetail, wild celery.

● **Tea and coffee substitutes.** The crushed leaves of hemlock, mint, raspberry and blackberry can be used to make wildwood teas, as can rose hips and the leaves of catnip, sweet goldenrod and the plant appropriately called New Jersey tea. These should be dried first, but wintergreen leaves are best used fresh. The dried flowers of the basswood tree and of red clover make good teas, as do boiled bits of sassafras root and bark. Also usable are: the leaves, flowers and stems of agrimony; the tips of lemon balm; meadowsweet, spearmint, sage and centaury.

The principal stand-ins for coffee are acorns, beechnuts and the roots of chicory and dandelion. The acorns and beechnuts must be ripe when gathered. Skin, cut into four and roast in a hot oven until they become cinnamon-brown in color; grind in a mill and put away in a tightly sealed container. The roots are washed, roasted in a slow oven until brittle, and ground in a coffee mill. The ripe seeds of the wild iris (yellow flag), roasted and ground, also make a fair coffee, as do the seeds of goose grass or cleavers, a variety of bedstraw. The leaves of a few species of evergreen holly in the Southeast contain caffein and can be boiled to make a beverage.

● **Syrup and sugar from tree saps.** The main syrup trees are the black and sugar maple; the red and white maples can also be tapped, but their yield is lower. The sap of each may be converted into wine by fermentation, or it may be evaporated to produce a syrup or a solid sugar. But it takes 40 gal. sap to make 1 gal. syrup, while the quantity of sap yielded by one tree in a season will seldom exceed 24 gal., and this amount of extraction may endanger the tree. The best trees are wide in the bole and with a good crown growth, a large full crown of leaves indicating large amounts of sweet sap.

Tap the tree at the time of its fullest sap flow, which is usually reckoned to begin with the spring thaw. Sap flow usually follows an alternation of warm days and frosty nights. To test for sap, break off a twig, and sap, if present, will exude. Tie a string to the twig guiding the drops of sap down into a bucket or a sealed plastic container. A gallon of sap will take 4–5 days to collect. Alternatively, make a ½-in. deep incision in the tree, slanting upwards, and gradually increase this to 2 in. Insert a spout through which the sap can flow into a bucket or a plastic bag hung beneath it in such a way that dirt and insects are kept out. Strain the liquid and boil it soon after collection to forestall fermentation. Use a shallow vessel, maintaining the depth of syrup at draw-off point at ½–1 in., and draw off the syrup as soon as it reaches its boiling temperature of 7° F above the boiling point of water. The syrup must be bottled hot, at 180° F or more.

Syrup is crystallized by raising its boiling point to 22° F or more above the boiling point of water; this releases more water and supersaturates the syrup which, when it cools to a room temperature of 68° F, will precipitate the excess sugar in the form of crystals. To help crystals to form, stir the hot solution continuously while it is cooling: this mixes the crystals throughout the thickened syrup and they grow in size and number.

Sugar may also be extracted by boiling from the sugar beet and mangel.

● **Edible fungi.** Fungi are a class of vegetables which, lacking chlorophyll, have to obtain their organic food ready made, either by using dead plant and animal products or by attaching themselves to living animals and plants as parasites. "Mushroom" is the name given to the fruiting body of the larger, fleshy fungi, particularly (though not exclusively) to those bearing gills, and more especially to those which are sought as food. Mushrooms vary in edibility from the delicious through the palatable and the unpleasant to the nauseous and deadly poisonous, and both esculent and poisonous varieties are to be found within the same genus. (The use of the word "toadstool" is meaningless and should be abandoned.) The food value of the mushroom is equal to that of most vegetables except that it contains rather more protein and makes up for the absence of vitamin C by possessing a large amount of vitamin B and the antirachitic vitamin D.

Some fungi are to be found from spring onwards, but fall is the main mushroom season. Mushrooms not wanted for use now may be strung on thread, dried slowly, and stored in glass jars, or made into ketchup.

● **Collecting mushrooms.**   Since it is impossible to get to know all the thousands of species of mushroom, the best course is to learn to recognize on sight about a dozen of the most common and flavorsome esculents, together with the commonest and deadliest of the poisonous kinds, of which there are few. There is no rule of thumb for sorting out poisonous from harmless varieties, and knowledge must be gotten by collecting specimens, taking them home and comparing them with the descriptions and pictures in a handbook such as *Mush-*

rooms, Edible and Otherwise: Habitat and Time of Growth by Myron Elisha Hard (1976) or *Some Common Mushrooms and How to Know Them* by Vera K. Charles, available from England.

Poisonous fungi. Because the most poisonous fungi all belong to the same genus, *Amanita*, they are not hard to recognize. They are: the death cap *(Amanita phalloides)*, the fool's mushroom *(A. verna)*, destroying angel *(A. virosa)*. It is their likeness to the common field mushroom which makes these fungi dangerous to the picker. Less dangerous because more easily recognizable is the fly agaric *(A. muscaria)*, which is rather decorative, with raised white spots on its red or brown caps.

● **Amanitas** are easily distinguished from edible mushrooms by these signs:

Amanitas	Mushrooms
Always have white gills.	May have white, pink, lilac, brown gills.
In early stage of growth have an egglike look, by reason of their being enveloped in a "universal veil."	Have no universal veil, only a partial veil leaving a ring below the cap when it is torn.
With growth, this veil tears, leaving the base of the stem sheathed with membrane called the "volva." All *Amanitas* have this volva.	No mushroom has a volva.

The rules for collecting fungi, therefore, resolve themselves into two: (1) reject any Mushroom which has white gills and a volva at the base of the stem; and (2) when in doubt, err on the side of caution. Most esculent fungi can be recognized easily with practice, and mistakes will at the most have uncomfortable rather than dangerous results.

● Descriptions of edible fungi.

Common field mushroom (Agaricus campestris). The best known of the wild species, having a whitish silky cap up to 4 in. across and gills that are first white, then pink, purple and blackish. White, smooth stem. Partial veil tears away to form annulus, or ring. Resembles the cultivated mushroom of the greengrocer's shop in appearance. Spores nearly chocolate brown.

Horse mushroom (A. arvensis). Similar in appearance to the above, but larger in size, and gills not pink.

Cep (Boletus edulis). Found on the ground in woods in autumn. Has a large, brown, rounded bunlike cap 3–8 in. across and a short, thick, often slightly bulbous stem 2½–6 in. long, often yellow-brown and marked with a network of raised lines on upper part. Its spores (which are yellow-olive) are produced in tubes rather than on the sides of gills. The flesh is thick and white. To dry for storage and use out of season, wipe ceps with a clean dry cloth, thread a needle with strong linen thread and string them on it. Hang in a cool oven (240° F) and after 24 hours remove and pack into glass jars. Cooking: Remove tubes and cut up flesh into slices. Fry in olive oil and season to taste.

Blewits (Tricholoma personatum). Grows among grass in pastures, often in large rings. Has a thick, rounded cap of pale brown color with a smooth surface 2½–5 in. across. A short, thick, fibrous stem, sometimes bulging at the base. Off-white or faintly pink gills often detached from the stem. The flesh is thick and firm, becoming spongy. White or salmon spores.

Wood blewits (T. nudum). Grows in woods, singly or in groups, in October/November. Cap is 2½–4 in. across, at first convex, becoming flat, lilac or lavender in color, including gills, which are rounded behind, sometimes nearly free of stem. Stem is 2–3 in. long and up to 1¼ in. thick, solid, bulging at base, at first blue, fading to lilac. The spores are flesh colored.

St. George's mushroom (T. gambosum). So called because it appears in England around 23 April (May in U.S.) in pastures, often in rings. It is of a sturdy appearance, buff in color, with a smooth cap 3–6 in. across, rounded and fleshy, with an incurved, wavy margin. Off-white to buff stem, short and stout, with white, downy apex. Gills are white to pale buff, with white spores. Cook slowly with a little butter, serve with white sauce.

Chantarelle (Cantharellus cibarius). Look for it in summer and autumn on the ground in woodland where it occurs singly or in groups and small clusters. It is crome- to egg-yellow in color with a smooth cap at first convex but later flattened and hollowed and at last funnel-shaped. Thick, firm flesh, with thick blunt-edged gills, sometimes foldlike, extending down the stem, of much the same color as the cap. When fresh, smells of prune. Spore is pinkish buff. Cooking: Wash very thoroughly, slice and cook in butter in a covered frying pan. When tender add parsley butter and a tablespoon or two of clear stock to form a little sauce. Mature specimens may be tough and will require slow cooking or stewing.

Saffron milk cap (Lactarius deliciosus). Found in damp woods and boggy places in July/November. The cap, up to 5 in. across, is orange or red with concentric zones of deeper color, later paling to gray or gray-green, at first convex then becoming funneled. The orange stem becomes green-spotted, is short and pithy, becoming hollow. When the gills or flesh of the cap or stem are broken a bright orange juice exudes, turning green on exposure. The flesh is pinkish orange, the spores pinkish-buff. Cooking: Grill rapidly and serve with a little butter, or use for flavouring soup. Does not dry well.

Parasol mushroom (Lepiota procera). Grows singly or in groups in open woods or pastures in summer and fall. At first resembling a drumstick, this large fungus expands to a parasol shape 3–5 in. across, with a marked central boss. The stem is very tall, tapering from its bulbous base, the cap covered with widely spaced brown scales, with white flesh beneath. The annulus can be moved up and down the stem; it is large and thick with brown scales underneath. The gills are white and free from the stem; the spores are white.

Fairy ring mushroom (Marasmius oreades). Found in grassy places, often growing in circles, from early spring to autumn. The cap is smooth, tough and brownish, 1–2 in. wide. It is first convex, then plane. The stem is 1–3 in. long, white and solid. They are best picked after a rain and can be sauteed, stewed, pickled, frozen or strung and dried for winter use.

Morel (Morchella esculenta). Found in spring in forest clearings and in hedges, orchards and pastures. Its distinctive spongelike head is grayish-brown to yellowish-brown, more or less elongated, its surface covered with irregular, rather elongated pits; its stalk is fragile, whitish in color and hollow. Cooking: Wash before use to remove all grit. Stuff with minced meat and bake in a casserole, or use as flavoring for soups and stews. Will dry.

Giant puffball (Calvatia gigantea). May be found in open woods, pastures and fields in autumn—a more or less globose growth, with a soft, white, leathery surface, attached to the ground by a short cord of root. Cooking: Cut in slices and fry.

When all these varieties are known at sight, and have been often gathered and eaten, it is safe to move on to other edible fungi, although those named above are by common consent the most worth gathering.

Cooking: Mushrooms generally can be baked in the oven, fried very slowly (using not too much butter) and grilled whole. They can be used in combination with other vegetables to make a dish (mushrooms and chestnuts, and mushrooms, tomatoes and green peas are good combinations), and as a flavoring for soups and stews.

● **Truffles** are far more common in Europe than in the United States but may occasionally be found here. The truffle is a black, warty, edible fungus which lives parasitically on the ailing roots of trees, about a foot under the ground. It prefers a light chalk soil and the roots of the oak but has also been found in association with beech, birch, chestnut and hornbeam roots. It is nearly globular in shape and somewhere between a walnut and a large potato in size. It cannot be cultivated or even encouraged and in its natural state is elusive. Its presence beneath a tree may be shown by the dying away of the herbage on the ground in a circular pattern around the tree which spreads gradually outwards; but even with this sign the precise position of the truffle must be found so that it can be dug up neatly without harm to a possible future crop. Sometimes the truffle betrays its presence by a faint cracking of the earth crust immediately above it, or in still winter days by the columns of gnats which hover just over the ground where it lies, attracted by its fragrance. The truffle is useless for food until it ripens, and so should only be dug for in the months between November and March.

Cooking. Wash and brush in water several times to remove all grit. Wrap separately in buttered paper and bake in a hot oven for one hour. Truffles are most commonly used in pâtés.

● **Mushroom poisoning.** Avoid giving alcohol to the patient. In all cases other than *Amanita* poisoning use an emetic and purgative to empty stomach and bowels of their contents. The antidote is oak bark in milk, which must be given before the poison has passed into the bloodstream. Prepare a decoction by boiling a handful of fresh or dried bark in 2 pints of milk. Give the patient plenty of sweet hot tea to drink, cold tea in the case of acrid Russula or milk caps; apply hot fomentations to abdominal pains.

□23□

BRIEF HERBAL

That the herbs of the field have biochemical properties which are capable of acting on the human organism in both beneficial and harmful ways has long been known.

Herbal medicines fall traditionally into ten categories corresponding to ten main types of physical need or discomfort.

Alternatives. Medicines which alter the condition of the body and improve general health. These include such blood-purifying herbs as burdock, bittersweet, stinging nettle, bitter dock.

Astringents. Medicines which produce contraction of the muscular fiber and in particular counteract looseness of the bowels. Blackberry, nettle, oak bark, plantain, witch hazel.

Carminatives. Medicines which aid digestion and relieve flatulence and stomachache. Angelica, balm, barberry, burdock, clover, wormwood.

Demulcents. Medicines which by a bland and soothing action allay irritation, especially in the case of inflammations of stomach and lungs. Agrimony, comfrey, linseed, marshmallow.

Diaphoretics. Medicines that are able to provoke perspiration, thus sweating out colds and fevers. Balm, catnip, yarrow.

Diuretics. Medicines which promote the discharge of urine. Asparagus, garlic, dandelion, Queen Anne's lace (wild carrot) bladderwrack (kelp), lily of the valley.

Emetics. Doses that induce vomiting. Mustard, salt.

Expectorants. Medicines that clear the chest, throat and lungs of phlegm. Horehound, bloodroot.

Laxatives. Preparations that loosen the bowels. Chickweed, dandelion, linseed, rhubarb.

Tonics. Medicines which give tone and vigor to the system. Balm, blackberry, camomile, centaury, gentian, hops, sage.

Herbal medicines, called "simples" when used singly, are normally taken internally in a decoction of the fresh or dried leaves, stems, flowers, berries or roots of the plant in question, often of the whole plant. Decoctions are made by covering the plant with boiling water and leaving it near the fire overnight to steep, the resulting liquid being poured off and used or bottled, the solids being thrown away unless required for use as a poultice. The following list is not meant to be more than a rough guide to ailments and some of their accepted remedies.

Anemia dandelion, nettle

Asthma coltsfoot, horehound, mullein, fireweed (willow herb)

Biliousness dandelion, groundsel (ragwort), strawberry

Bladder trouble couch grass, dandelion, balm

Boils chickweed, ground ivy, yarrow

Bronchial trouble clover, coltsfoot, ground ivy, bloodroot, sunflower seeds, linseed

Catarrh clover, ground ivy, boneset (thoroughwort)

Chapped skin groundsel, silverweed (ext.)*

Chilblains onion and salt (ext.)

Colds, chills dead nettle, yarrow, fireweed

Constipation chickweed, dandelion, groundsel

Coughs clover, ground ivy, linseed, horehound, speedwell

Cramp mustard, pennyroyal, saxifrage (ext.)

Cystitis couch grass, marshmallow

Diarrhea blackberry leaves, oak bark, comfrey root

Dyspepsia dandelion, ground ivy, mint, horseradish

Eczema dandelion, walnut leaves and bark, watercress (ext.)

Eye lotions chickweed, ground ivy, eyebright, sarsaparilla, sassafras

Flatulence clover, dandelion, ground ivy, wormwood

Foot discomfort bedstraw (cleavers), silverweed (ext.)

Gallstones couch grass, sow thistle, silverweed, cascara sagrada (bitter bark)

Gout cinquefoil, couch grass, dandelion, ground ivy, nettle, carrot, chicory root, burdock

Gravel couch grass, dandelion, nettle

Insomnia lettuce, privet

Jaundice couch grass, ground ivy, yarrow, thyme, lady's mantle

Kidney trouble clover, couch grass, sage, dandelion, parsley, thyme

Liver trouble dandelion, dock, maple leaf or bark, sage

Neuralgia poppy heads, camomile

Obesity bladderwrack, chickweed

Piles celandine, elder, blackberry, witch hazel

Pulmonary complaints ground ivy, comfrey, bloodroot

Rheumatism couch grass, nettle, celery seed, bladderwrack, comfrey, chicory root, birthwort

Sciatica ground ivy, juniper berry

Skin eruptions dandelion, figwort (ext.)

Sprains and bruises witch hazel (ext.)

Stomach upset chickweed, oak bark, lemon verbena

Stone in bladder lady's mantle

Throat, relaxed, sore, ulcerated herbs of *Potentilla* genus, nettle, bloodroot

Ulcers and wounds comfrey, marigold, self-heal, wintergreen, slippery elm, plantain, loosestrife (ext.)

Varicose veins daisy (ext.)

Warts milk of dandelion, celandrine, lining of broad bean shell (ext.)

Whooping cough clover

* (ext.) indicates external application.

SOME FURTHER USES OF HERBS

Elder. A bush of common elder outside a kitchen window keeps away flies.

Sage. Some leaves of sage burned on a shovel or plate destroy odors.

Marigold. The petals of the ray florets are used to flavor buns, soups, stews. May be used to color butter and cheese.

Parsley. A purifier of the breath after smoking or eating onion or garlic.

Marjoram.   Lay a sprig of marjoram across a milk jug to keep milk fresh.

Sloe.   The juice of a ripe sloe is an effective marking ink: stick nib into the fruit and write.

Lady's bedstraw.   Also called yellow bedstraw or cleavers, or cheese rennet because it has the property of curdling milk.

Soapwort (bouncing Bet).   Both root and leaves contain saponin. "Bruised and agitated with water, it raises a lather like a soap, which easily washes dirty spots out of clothes."—Culpeper. Some species of the genus *Gypsophila* contain much saponin, which is also to be found in horse chestnuts.

Tansy, rue and mint.   All these deter flies.

Poisonous herbs: Anemone, aconite, belladonna (deadly nightshade), Indian poke (false hellebore), hemlock, cowbane, jimsonweed (thorn apple).

WEIGHTS, MEASURES & TEMPERATURES

Length

1 inch	= 2.5400 centimers (cm)
1 foot	= 0.3048 meters (m)
1 yard	= 0.9144 m
1 rod	= 5.0292 m
1 chain	= 20.117 m
1 furlong	= 201.17 m
1 mile	= 1.6093 kilometers (km)

Surface or Area

1 sq inch	= 6.451 sq cm
1 sq foot	= 0.0929 sq m
1 sq yard	= 0.8361 sq m
1 acre	= 4.047 sq m
1 sq mile	= 2.590 sq km

Volume

1 cu inch	= 16.387 cu cm
1 cu foot	= 0.0283 cu m
1 cu yard	= 0.7646 cu m

Capacity

1 pint	= 0.4732 liters
1 quart	= 0.9463 liters
1 gallon	= 3.7854 liters
1 bushel	= 35.239 liters

Weight, avoirdupois

1 ounce	= 28.350 grams (g)
1 pound	= 0.4536 kilograms (kg)
1 ton	= 0.9072 metric tons

°Centigrade	°Fahrenheit	°Centigrade	°Fahrenheit
100	212	36.7	98
95	203	35	95
90	194	32.2	90
85	185	30	86
78.9	174	26.7	80
75	167	25	77
70	158	20	68
65	149	15.5	60
60	140	12.8	55
55	131	10	50
52.8	127	7.2	45
50	122	5	41
45	113	1.7	35
42.2	108	0	32
40	104		

APPENDIX I SOURCES OF AGRICULTURAL INFORMATION FOR YOUR AREA.

Agricultural Information
Auburn Univ.
Auburn, Alabama 36830

Agricultural Information
Univ. of Alaska
College, Alaska 99701

Agricultural Information
College of Agriculture
Univ. of Arizona
Tucson, Arizona 85721

Agricultural Information
Univ. of Arkansas
P.O. Box 391
Little Rock, Arkansas 72203

Agricultural Information
Agricultural Ext. Service
2200 University Ave.
Berkeley, California 94720

Agricultural Information
Colorado State Univ.
Fort Collins, Colorado 80521

Agricultural Information
College of Agriculture
Univ. of Connecticut
Storrs, Connecticut 06268

Agricultural Information
College of Agricultural Sciences
Univ. of Delaware
Newark, Delaware 19711

Agricultural Information
Univ. of Florida
217 Rolfs Hall
Gainesville, Florida 32601

Agricultural Information
College of Agriculture
Univ. of Georgia
Athens, Georgia 30602

Agricultural Information
Univ. of Hawaii
2500 Dole St.
Honolulu, Hawaii 96822

Agricultural Information
College of Agriculture

Univ. of Idaho
Moscow, Idaho 83843

Agricultural Information
College of Agriculture
Univ. of Illinois
Urbana, Illinois 61801

Agricultural Information
Agricultural Administration
    Bldg.
Purdue Univ.
Lafayette, Indiana 47907

Agricultural Information
Iowa State Univ.
Ames, Iowa 50010

Agricultural Information
Kansas State Univ.
Manhattan, Kansas 66502

Agricultural Information
College of Agriculture
Univ. of Kentucky
Lexington, Kentucky 40506

Agricultural Information
Louisiana State Univ.
Knapp Hall, Univ. Station
Baton Rouge, Louisiana 70803

Agricultural Information
Dept. of Public Information
Univ. of Maine
Orono, Maine 04473

Agricultural Information
Univ. of Maryland
Agricultural Division

College Park, Maryland 20742

Agricultural Information
Stockbridge Hall
Univ. of Massachusetts
Amherst, Massachusetts 01002

Agricultural Information
Dept. of Information Services
109 Agricultural Hall
East Lansing, Michigan 48823

Department of Information
Institute of Agriculture
Univ. of Minnesota
St. Paul, Minnesota 55101

Agricultural Information
Mississippi State Univ.
State College, Mississippi 39762

Agricultural Information
I-98 Agricultural Bldg.
Univ. of Missouri
Columbia, Missouri 65201

Office of Information
Montana State Univ.
Bozeman, Montana 59715

Department of Information
College of Agriculture
Univ. of Nebraska
Lincoln, Nebraska 68503

Agricultural Communications
    Service
Univ. of Nevada
Reno, Nevada 89507

Agricultural Information
Schofield Hall
Univ. of New Hampshire
Durham, New Hampshire
03824

Agricultural Information
College of Agriculture
Rutgers, The State Univ.
New Brunswick, New Jersey
08903

Agricultural Information
Drawer 3A1
New Mexico State Univ.
Las Cruces, New Mexico 88001

Agricultural Information
State College of Agriculture
Cornell Univ.
Ithaca, New York 13850

Agricultural Information
North Carolina State Univ.
State College Station
Raleigh, North Carolina 27607

Agricultural Information
North Dakota State Univ.
State Univ. Station
Fargo, North Dakota 58102

Cooperative Extension Service
The Ohio State Univ.
2120 Fyffe Road
Columbus, Ohio 43210

Agricultural Information
Oklahoma State Univ.

Stillwater, Oklahoma 74074

Agricultural Information
206 Waldo Hall
Oregon State Univ.
Corvallis, Oregon 97331

Agricultural Information
The Pennsylvania State Univ.
Room 1, Armsby Bldg.
University Park, Pennsylvania
16802

Cooperative Ext. Service
Univ. of Puerto Rico
Mayaguez Campus, P.O. Box AR
Rio Piedras, Puerto Rico 00928

Agricultural Information
Univ. of Rhode Island
16 Woodwall Hall
Kingston, Rhode Island 02881

Agricultural Information
Clemson Univ.
Clemson, South Carolina 29631

Agricultural Information
South Dakota State Univ.
Univ. Station
Brookings, South Dakota 57006

Agricultural Information
Univ. of Tennessee
P.O. Box 1071
Knoxville, Tennessee 37901

Department of Agricultural
Information

Services Bldg.
Texas A & M Univ.
College Station, Texas 77843

Agricultural Information
Utah State Univ.
Logan, Utah 84321

Agricultural Information
Univ. of Vermont
Burlington, Vermont 05401

Agricultural Information
Virginia Polytechnic Institute
Blacksburg, Virginia 24061

Agricultural Information
115 Wilson Hall
Washington State Univ.
Pullman, Washington 99163

Agricultural Information
Evansdale Campus
Appalachian Center
West Virginia Univ.
Morgantown, West Virginia
26506

Agricultural Information
Univ. of Wisconsin
Madison, Wisconsin 53706

Agricultural Information
Univ. of Wyoming
P.O. Box 3354
Laramie, Wyoming 82070

Information Services
Federal Ext. Service
U.S. Department of Agriculture
Washington, D.C. 20250

APPENDIX II   FISH AND GAME DEPARTMENTS OF THE UNITED STATES AND CANADA

When writing for information, address queries to Director, Information and Education.

UNITED STATES

Alabama Department of Conservation and
    Natural Resources
64 North Union Street
Montgomery 36104 (205–269–7221)

Alaska Department of Fish and Game
Subport Building
Juneau 99801 (907–586–3392)

Arizona Game and Fish Department
2222 West Greenway Road
Phoenix 85023 (602–942–3000)

Arkansas Game and Fish Commission
Game and Fish Building
Little Rock 72201 (501–371–1145)

California Department of Fish and Game
The Resources Agency

1416 9th Street
Sacramento 95814 (916–445–3531)

Colorado Department of Natural Resources
Division of Wildlife
6060 Broadway
Denver 80216 (303–825–1192)

Connecticut Department of Environmental
    Protection
State Office Building
Hartford 06115 (203–566–5460)

Delaware Department of Natural Resources
    and Environmental Control
Division of Fish and Wildlife
D Street
Dover 19901 (302–678–4431)

District of Columbia Metropolitan Police
300 Indiana Avenue, N.W.
Washington 20001 (202–626–2305)

Florida Department of Natural
    Resources
620 South Meridian
Tallahassee 32304
    (904–488–2972)

Georgia State Game and Fish Division
Trinity-Washington Building
270 Washington Street, S.W.
Atlanta 30334 (404–656–3500)

Guam Department of Agriculture
Division of Fish and Wildlife
Agana 96910 (772–6866)

Hawaii Department of Land and Natural
  Resources
Division of Fish and Game
1179 Punchbowl Street
Honolulu 96813 (548–4000)

Idaho Fish and Game
  Department
600 South Walnut, Box 25
Boise 83707 (208–384–3771)

Illinois Department of Conservation
State Office Building
Springfield 62706 (217–525–6302)

Indiana Department of Natural Resources
Division of Fish and Wildlife
608 State Office Building
Indianapolis 46204 (317–633–6344)

Iowa State Conservation Commission
State Office Building
300 4th Street
Des Moines 50319 (515–281–5384)

Kansas Forestry, Fish and Game
  Commission
Box 1028
Pratt 67124 (316–672–6473)

Kentucky Department of Fish and Wildlife
  Resources
Capitol Plaza Tower
Frankfort 40601 (502–564–3400)

Louisiana Wildlife and Fisheries
  Commission

P.O. Box 44095
Capitol Station
Baton Rouge 70804

Maine Department of Inland Fisheries and
   Game
State Office Building
Augusta 04330 (207–289–3371)

Maryland Fisheries Administration
Natural Resources Department
State Office Building
Annapolis 21401 (301–367–5558)

Massachusetts Department of Natural
   Resources
100 Cambridge Street
Boston 02202 (617–727–3151)

Michigan Department of Natural Resources
Mason Building
Lansing 48926 (517–373–1220)

Minnesota Department of Natural
   Resources
Division of Game and Fish
301 Centennial Building
658 Cedar Street
St. Paul 55101 (612–296–2894)

Mississippi Game and Fish Commission
Robert E. Lee Office Building
239 North Lamar Street
P.O. Box 451
Jackson 39205 (601–354–7333)

Missouri Department of Conservation
P.O. Box 180
Jefferson City 65101 (314–751–4115)

Montana Fish and Game Department
Helena 59601 (406–449–3186)

Nebraska Game and Parks Commission
P.O. Box 30370
2200 North 33rd
Lincoln 68503 (402–434–0641

Nevada Department of Fish and Game
Box 10678
Reno 89510 (702–784–6214)

New Hampshire Fish and Game
Department
34 Bridge Street
Concord 03301 (603–271–3421)

New Jersey Department of Environmental
Protection
Division of Fish, Game, and Shellfisheries
Box 1390
Trenton 08625 (609–292–2965)

New Mexico Department of Game and Fish
State Capitol
Santa Fe 87501 (505–827–2143)

New York Department of Environmental
Conservation
Fish and Wildlife Division
50 Wolf Road
Albany 12201 (518–457–5690)

North Carolina Wildlife Resources
Commission
325 North Salisbury Street
Raleigh 27611 (919–829–3391)

North Dakota State Game and Fish
  Department
2121 Lovett Avenue
Bismarck 58501 (701–224–2180)

Ohio Department of Natural Resources
Division of Wildlife
Fountain Square
Columbus 43224 (614–466–4603)

Oklahoma Department of Wildlife
  Conservation
1801 North Lincoln
P.O. Box 53465
Oklahoma City 73105 (405–521–3851)

Oregon Fish Commission
307 State Office Building
Portland 97201 (503–229–5671)

Oregon State Wildlife Commission
Box 3503
Portland 97208 (503–229–5551)

Pennsylvania Fish Commission
P.O. Box 1673
Harrisburg 17120 (717–787–6593)

Pennsylvania Game Commission
P.O. Box 1567
Harrisburg 17120 (717–787–3633)

Puerto Rico Department of Natural
  Resources
P.O. Box 11488
San Juan 00910

Rhode Island Department of Natural
  Resources

Division of Fish and Wildlife
83 Park Street
Providence 02903 (401–277–2784)

South Carolina Wildlife Resources
  Department
Box 167
1015 Main Street
Columbia 29202 (803–758–2561)

South Dakota Department of Game, Fish
  and Parks
State Office Building
Pierre 57501 (605–224–3381)

Tennessee Wildlife Resources Agency
Box 40747
Ellington Agricultural Center
Nashville 37220 (615–741–1431)

Tennessee Wildlife Resources Agency
Box 40747
Ellington Agricultural Center
Nashville 37220 (615–741–1431)

Texas Parks and Wildlife Department
John H. Reagan Building
Austin 78701 (512–475–2087)

Utah State Department of Natural
  Resources
Division of Wildlife Resources
1596 W.N. Temple
Salt Lake City 84116 (801–328–5081)

Vermont Agency of Environmental
  Conservation
Fish and Game Department
Montpelier 05602 (802–828–3371)

Virginia Commission of Game and Inland
   Fisheries
4010 West Broad Street
Box 11104
Richmond 23230 (804–770–4974)

Washington Department of Fisheries
115 General Administration Building
Olympia 98504 (206–753–6623)

Washington Department of Game
600 North Capitol Way
Olympia 98504 (206–753–5700)

West Virginia Department of Natural
   Resources
1800 Washington Street
East Charleston 25305 (304–348–2754)

Wisconsin Department of Natural
   Resources
Box 450
Madison 53701 (608–266–2243)

Wyoming Game and Fish Department
Box 1589
Cheyenne 82001 (307–777–7631)

CANADA

Alberta Department of Lands and Forests
Natural Resources Building
Edmonton T5K 2E1 (403–229–4461)

British Columbia Department of Recreation
   and Conservation
Fish and Wildlife Branch
Parliament Buildings
Victoria (604–387–6409)

Manitoba Department of Mines
Resources and Environmental Management
Box 18
139 Tuxedo Boulevard
Winnipeg R3M 0H6 (204–786–7931)

New Brunswick Department of Natural
    Resources
Fish and Wildlife Branch
Fredericton (506–453–2433)

Newfoundland Department of Tourism
Wildlife Division
Confederation Building
St. John's (709–722–0711, Ext. 327)

A COUNTRY GLOSSARY

acre   area of land containing 4,840 sq. yd. or 160 sq. rods (see *chain*)

adze   ax-edged, hoe-shaped tool for rough-hollowing timber

afterbirth   the placenta and that part of the fetal membranes that are discharged from the uterus after the birth of offspring

aggregate   any coarser material mixed with cement to form concrete

anaerobic   change effected by the agency of bacteria living in the absence of free oxygen

annual   plant that completes its life history in one year

antirachitic   opposing or peventing the development of rickets

arable   land under cultivation and used mainly for cropping

artesian well   well sunk in a valley or "basin" under conditions which ensure that water rises and discharges at the surface with some force

bale   straw of hay compressed and bound in rectangular block

barm   froth of fermenting liquor

barrow   male pig castrated before it becomes sexually active.

baste   to pour fat over (a joint of meat)

bat   stout stick

batter inward slope from perpendicular

battery a series of cages for raising or fattening poultry

beebread stored pollen in comb

beetle large wood mallet used for driving stakes and splitting timber

beeves cattle, oxen

besom a rough broom of twigs

biennial plant which completes its life history in 2 years

billet thick piece of split log

bin container for grain. To find capacity of a bin in bushels, multiply length by width by depth in feet, and multiply by (roughly, 0.803).

bine the stem of common hop varieties

bole trunk of tree between soil level and lower branches

bran outer skin of wheat grain

brassica cruciferous plant of the genus *Brassica* (cabbages, turnips, mustards, cauliflower, rape, etc.

brawn a product made from chopped, cooked and edible parts of a pig's head, feet, legs and sometimes tongue

brewer's grains spent grains after extraction of malt, fed to stock

brine salt in water solution (1 percent salt in brine = 1 oz. salt per gal water; 10 percent = 14 oz; 15 percent = 22½ oz.)

broaches pegs used in thatching

broadcast to scatter or sow seed widely and in all directions

brock swill

broil to grill, or cook over hot coals

bull uncastrated male of the cattle family

bullock castrated male cattle

bung the stopper of a cask

bushel measure of capacity used especially for grain, measuring 2150.42 cu. in. and containing about 78 lb. or 10 gal. water.

In dry measure the bushel contains 32 quarts. A bushel of wheat contains 60 lb., rye 56 lb., sweet corn 50 lb., barley 60 lb. and oats 32 lb.

callus tissue that forms over a cut surface of plant stem or root

campden tablet sterilizing agent (potassium metabisulphite) used in fruit preserving and wine making

cast the distance a bow can shoot

catch crop crop grown quickly between two main crops

cesspool system of disposing of sewage by underground storage in tank which must be periodically emptied

chaff fine-cut straw or hay used as food for livestock

chain 22 yd. or 100 links. 10 chains = 1 furlong, or "long furrow," the distance an ox could plough without resting, and therefore the most common length of a field. There are 10 sq. chains in 1 acre. If an oblong field is 5½ by 6¾ chains, to find its area multiply 5.5 by 6.75 = 37.125 chains or 3.7125 acres—approximately 3¾ acres.

cleave to split wood along the grain

cloche a translucent cover for a young plant or shoot

cock an adult male domestic fowl

cockerel a young male domestic fowl

cold frame an outdoor shallow rectangular frame of boards or concrete with a cover, usually glass, to protect small plants from wind and low temperature, especially early in the growing season

concentrate protein- and oil-rich rations for stock

colter metal cutting edge of ploughshare

coney a rabbit or rabbit fur

coppice, copse a small wood from which timber is systematically cut for use

cord 128 cu ft (of timber); roughly, a pile of logs 8 ft by 4 ft by 4 ft

cordwood tree branches cut from trunk of felled tree

corm   a solid, swollen underground stem

course   system of rotation cropping to suit soil of a particular district

creep feeder   arrangement which allows food to be fed to young pigs to the exclusion of the mother sow

crowbar   iron bar shaped for use as a tool

cull   to pick out weak specimens of stock

curtilage   yards and premises about the house

dam   female parent of animal

dead stock   farm tools and quipment, as distinct from animals

dead weight   weight of carcass

deciduous   trees which lose their leaves annually

decorticated   nut meal from which the fibrous cortex has been removed

Devonshire cream   cream allowed to rise on milk, set by heating and then cooling, and skimmed from the underlying skim milk

dogs   iron stands, or andirons, over which logs are laid for burning

doles or nibs   handles attached to scythe shaft

dowse   to locate water underground by means of involuntary muscular movement communicated to a rod held in dowser's hands

drake   male duck

draw   to remove the innards of an animal; to eviscerate

drench   medicine for animal; to administer such

dress   to clean corn of impurities; to prepare food animals by bleeding and cleaning

drey   nest of squirrel

drill   a shallow furrow or trench into which seed is sown; an implement that makes such furrows and sows seed into them; to sow seed in drills

drystone   stone-built without mortar

ensilage *silage,* q.v.

espalier a fruit tree or other plant trained to grow flat against a building wall, railing, trellis or other support

fallow land left unsown to recover after cropping

farrow litter of pigs

filly young female horse

fine to clear a wine of floating particles

flitch side of bacon

fodder food supplied to cattle and horses

form the resting place of a hare

froe woodcutting tool with blade set at right angles to handle

furlong see *chain*

gaff fisherman's hooked pole

gallon liquid measure = 4 quarts = 8 pints = 231 cu. in. = 3.785 liters. 1 gal. water weighs about 8 lb.

game wild animals hunted for sport

gander male goose

gelding castrated male horse

gilt young sow

grist malt after grinding

ground bait bait scattered on the water to attract fish

harden off to inure to cold or other unfavorable environmental conditions by gradual exposure to lower temperatures, by decreasing the water supply, etc.

hardwood timber from deciduous trees

haulm (dried) stem and leaves of long-stemmed plants

head (of water) energy owing to height, velocity and pressure

heat period of estrus in female animal

heifer young cow

helve ax handle

herdbook official record of the individuals and pedigrees of a breed of especially cattle or swine

hinny   hydrid of horse and female ass

hog   a domestic swine

hoggin   a soft coarse red sand

hogshead   cask of 63-gal. capacity

hoven   bloat; distention of stomach of grazing animal by gas

humus   decomposed organic matter in topsoil

keeping   of or relating to something that remains unspoiled over a period of time

kerf   cut made by saw-teeth

kibbled   coarsely milled (grain)

kindle   to bring forth young (used chiefly of rabbits)

lactation   coming into milk of female animal

lateral   side shoot of plant

lees   sediment in wine

legumes   plants bearing pods, e.g. beans, peas

let-down   a physiological response of lactating mammals to suckling or similar pressure which causes milk to flow downward where it can be drawn from the nipple

leveret   young hare

ley   arable land under grass or pasture

light   a glazed frame

litter   straw for floor

loam   the top 6 in. of pasture

lye   strong alkali solution

marc   the pressed pulp in cider, wine or oil making

market gardening   cultivation of a fairly extensive area to produce vegetables for sale on the market

mast   the fruit of beech, oak, chestnut and other forest trees

middlings   coarser part of wheat left after sieving

milch   bred or suitable for milk production as distinct from other uses

mild steel   a low-carbon steel that is soft and easily worked and is used for construction purposes

moldboard   part of plough that turns over the furrow

monkey winch   machine with winch and lever used to grub up tree stumps

mortar   (soft) lime and sand mixed with water; (cement) portland cement mixed with sand and water. For bricklaying, use 1 part cement to 4 parts bricklaying sand. Wet bricks before using.

mucking out   removing dung from stable, coop, etc.

mulch   straw, peat or compost laid at the roots of plants to conserve moisture

mule   neuter hybrid between mare and male ass

must   juice expressed from fruit before fermentation into wine

night soil   human excrement in raw state

osier   willow which yields rods for basket making

ox   male or female of common domestic cattle, especially a castrated male

pan, hardpan   hard layer of soil at level of repeated cultivation

pasture   land left under grass for grazing of livestock

paunch   to eviscerate, disembowel

peck   ¼ bushel

pelt   skin of small furred animal

pen   a number of animals regarded as a suitable unit for breeding

pike   a pile of hay or grain having a pointed top

pluck   the lungs, heart, liver, windpipe and gullet of a slaughtered animal

pomace   crushed apples for cider

pony   small horse, less than 14 hands high

porker   pig raised for table use as fresh pork and having 60–80 lb. dead weight

puddle   an earthy mixture (as of clay, sand and gravel) worked while wet into a compact mass that becomes impervious to water when dry

prove   allow dough to rise by the action of carbonic acid gas

pullet   young fowl on point of lay, or just laying

punk   touchwood, wood decayed by fungal attack

rack   to draw off (wine) from lees

registered   recorded in herdbook, q.v.

render   to extract by melting; to apply a coat (i.e., of plaster or cement) directly to

rennet   a preparation of the lining membrane of the stomach of animals that is used for curdling milk

rick   an elongated stack or pile (as of grain, straw or hay) in the open air and often protected from the wet with thatching

riparian   of a river bank

riprap   a foundation or sustaining wall of stones, bricks, cement, and rubble thrown together without order

rod   5½ yd. (length of oxgoad)

rodent   gnawing animal with front teeth that continue growing throughout animal's life

roguing   eliminating inferior specimens, in plant breeding

rotation   systematic annual change of ground for specific crops

runt   the poor pig in a litter

saddle   the undivided loins of a carcass prepared for roasting

Scotch hands   a pair of small paddles for working butter

scurf   flaky material that becomes detached from the epidermis

scion   part of a tree, jointed to a rootstock of more vigorous growth in grafting

score   20 lb. weight of a pig

screen   to put through a sieve

season   to leave timber in open to dry out before use: allow 1 year for each inch thickness of planks.

septic tank   system of disposing of sewage from bathrooms through anaerobic bacterial action

serve   to impregnate female animal

set   badger's lair; a young plant or rooted cutting or tuber ready for setting out

shard   gap in a hedge

share   blade of plough

shock   a pile of usually eight to sixteen sheaves of grain set up in a field butt end down, often with one or two of the sheaves broken over the top to serve as a protection against weather

shoddy   an inferior grade of wool

silage   fodder made by fermentation of green cops in a silo

simple   medicinal herb

sire   male animal used for breeding

slake   to hydrate, as lime

slurry   solids mixed with water

small fruit   a low-growing plant that produces table fruits (as the strawberry, raspberry, currant)

snath   stem of scythe

sod   clump of grass with soil

soil   to feed stock with greenstuff cut straight from field or garden

sow   mature female pig

squab   young pigeon raised for food

stallion   uncastrated male horse

steer   young bullock

stool   a stump or stand of plants from which shoots sprout

swath   one sweep with a scythe; the line of mown hay

tallow   beef or mutton fat rendered in boiling water

tether   to fasten an animal by means of harness, chain and stake

tilt   canvas or tarpaulin cover

tine   prong of fork or harrow

trail   entrail

trivet   three-legged stand with a handle, placed in embers to support kettle or pot

tuber   fleshy underground stem

tun   a brewer's fermentation vat

vent   anus, especially of a fish or bird

vermin   all obnoxious insects, animals and birds

weaner   a young animal weaned from its mother

wether   castrated ram

withe   a flexible slender twig or branch

wort   unfermented, or fermenting malt

yard   (of gravel, sand) 27 cu. ft.

BIBLIOGRAPHY

COHAN, RAY. *How to Make It on the Land.* New York: Galahad Books, 1972.

LOGSDON, GENE. *Homesteading: HOW TO Find New Independence on the Land.* Emmaus, PA: Rodale Press, Inc., 1973.

SMITH, W.G. *Gardening for Food.* New York: Charles Scribner's Sons, 1972.

The Mother Earth News, 105 Stoney Mountain Road, Hendersonville, NC. January 1977 to current issue.

LANGER, RICHARD W. *Grow It!* The Beginner's Complete In-Harmony-with-Nature Small Farm Guide, from Vegetable and Grain growing to Livestock Care. New York: Avon, 1972.

FOSTER, CATHARINE OSGOOD. The Organic Gardener. New York: Vintage, 1972.

CARLETON, R. MILTON. The New Vegetable & Fruit Garden Book. Chicago: Henry Regnery, 1976.

LAUREL, ALICIA BAY. Living on the Earth. New York: Vintage, 1971.

GIBBONS, EUELL. Stalking the Wild Asparagus. New York: David McKay, 1962.

SPARANO, VIN T. Complete Outdoors Encyclopedia. New York: Harper and Row, 1972.

BARTON, BILL, ed. The Sportsman's Encyclopedia. New York: Grosset and Dunlap, 1971.

SAMSON, JACK. The Sportsman's World. New York: Holt, Rinehart & Winston, 1976.

SAND, GEORGE R. The Complete Beginner's Guide to Fishing. New York: Doubleday & Co., 1974.

US FISH AND WILDLIFE SERVICE. Issuance of Annual Regulations Permitting the Sport Hunting of Migratory Birds, Department of the Interior Draft Environmental Statement, np, nd (but with 1974–75 regulations).

STRUNG, NORMAN. The Hunter's Almanac. New York, MacMillan Co., 1971.

DuBROFF, SIDNEY. Shooting, Fishing and Gun Book. Hampshire, GB: Spur Publications, 1976. (including sections on hunting and fishing in US)

ANGIER, BRADFORD. Wilderness Cookery. Harrisburg, PA: The Stackpole Co., 1961.

HARTE, JOHN, AND ROBERT H. SOCOLOW. Patient Earth. New York: Holt, Rinehart & Winston, 1971.

US DEPARTMENT OF AGRICULTURE. 1973 Yearbook of Agriculture: Handbook for the Home. Washington, DC: GPO.

WALL, ROY. Fish and Game Cookery. New York: M.S. Mill Co., 1945.

DAVIS, J. CHARLES II. Fish Cookery, NY: A.S. Barnes & Co., 1967.

DeGOUY, L.P. The Derrydale Cook Book of Fish and Game. New York: Derrydale Press, 1937.

MILORADOVICH, MILO. The Art of Fish Cookery. New York: Doubleday & Co., 1949.

BILES, ROY E. The Complete Illustrated Book of Garden Magic. Chicago: J.G. Ferguson Publishing Co., 1969.

HARD, MYRON ELISHA. Mushrooms, Edible and Otherwise: Habitat and Time of Growth. New York: Dover.

PETERSON, ROGER TORY. A Field Guide to the Birds. Boston: Houghton Mifflin Co., 1949.

BURKE, EDMUND H. Archery Handbook. New York: Arco, 1976.

McILNAY, ANNABELLE. Making Wine at Home. Secaucus, NJ: Citadel Press, 1974.

BERGLUND, BERNDT, AND CLARE E. BOLDE. The Edible Wild: A Complete Cookbook and Guide to the Edible Wild Plants in Canada and Eastern North America. New York: Charles Scribner's Sons, 1971.

RICKETT, HAROLD WILLIAM. The New Field Book of American Wild Flowers. NY: G.P. Putnam's Sons, 1963.

KADANS, JOSEPH M. Modern Encyclopedia of Herbs. West Nyack, NY: Parker Publishing Co., Inc., 1970.

EVERARD, BARBARA (paintings) and Morley, Brian D. (text). Wild Flowers of the World. London: Ebury Press and Michael Joseph, 1970.

ABEL, BOB. The Book of Beer. Chicago: Henry Regnery, 1976.

KRAMER, JACK. The Free Earth Guide to Gardening. New York, Walker and Company, 1974.